THE SALMON
&
SEA TROUT
FISHER'S HANDBOOK

FLIES THAT HAVE CAUGHT SALMON

Munro Killer
12lb, R.Spey
May 1988

Spencer's Pool Fly
17 lb, R. Gaula
June 1992

Silver Willie Gunn
16lb, R. Tyne
September 1992

Thunder Stoat
8lb, R. Lune
October 1996

Silver Stoat
7lb, R.Dee
August 1992

Yellow Dog
(Polar Bear)
9lb, R. Bush
March 1995

Stuart Special
12lb, R. Spey
July 1993

Polar Bear Shrimp
14lb, R.Ribble
October 1995

Silver Spider
9lb, R.Hodder
October 1988

Thunder Stoat
6lb, 5lb, R.Dee (Sc)
August 1993

Orange Shrimp
7lb, 22lb, R. Nith
November 1987

Munro Killer
18lb, R. Lune
September 1989

Teal, Blue & Silver
9lb, R. Lune
June 1989

Silver Stoat
5lb, R. Drowse
August 1990

Thunder Stoat
11lb, R. Tay
Septemeber 1988

Blue Charm
8lb, 13lb, R. Annan
November 1988

Silver Rat
20lb, 14lb, 6lb, R.Nith
September 1989

Munro Killer
15lb, R. Hodder
October 1995

Polar Bear Tube
(aluminium)
17lb, R. Eden
February 1988

Orange & Blue Tube
(brass)
20lb, R. Eden
March 1979

Yellow Dog Tube
(aluminium)
37lb, R. Alta
August 1992

THE SALMON
&
SEA TROUT
FISHER'S HANDBOOK

HUGH FALKUS & MALCOLM GREENHALGH

EXCELLENT PRESS

LUDLOW

Excellent Press
Palmers House
7 Corve Street
Ludlow
Shropshire SY8 1DB

First published 1997

A copy of the British Library cataloguing in Publication Data for this title is
available from the British Library.

Book and cover design by Mary Hamlyn, Hamlyn Design, Ludlow.

ISBN 1 900318 04 0

Printed and bound in the E. C.

ACKNOWLEDGMENTS

The completion of this book would not have been possible without the support and encouragement of many friends and loved ones, especially Kathleen Falkus, Yvonne my wife, Bill Arnold, Stuart Butcher, Michael Daunt, Alan Davies, Dave Evans, Bob Fitchie, Peter Greenhalgh, Geoff Haslam, Chris Heap, Brian Hoggarth, Jack Morris, Albert Sanderson, Paul Stanton, Brian Wells and the members of Bowland Game-Fishing Association.

Arthur Oglesby provided unique photographs from HF's earlier days; Tom Rawling's articles and photographs are reproduced by kind permission of his daughters and *Trout & Salmon* magazine. Photographs taken especially for the book are by Jason Smalley. Denys Ovenden's delightful drawings have enhanced the text. Raymond Rocher, the famous French angler, kindly sent details of nymph fishing for salmon on the River Test . The vastness of the Baltic is dramatically captured in a photograph provided by Columbus Leth of Copenhagen. Elizabeth and James Williams sent deadly flies from Devonshire. John Mitchell of Normark - Rapala provided Cortland fly lines and Rapala lures, Partridge of Redditch the finest of hooks, and David Norwich and Bruce & Walker some superb salmon and sea trout rods.

Publishers are often overlooked but David Burnett, who has nurtured this book since its conception, cannot be. His contribution is as great as anyone's - in all aspects. To all these helpers who have contributed in so many ways to making Hugh's 'Till Book' a reality I extend my thanks.

Malcolm Greenhalgh

FLY-FISHING CHECKLIST

1　Rods
2　Reels with appropriate fly-lines
3　Leaders
4　Darning needle
5　Fly box
6　Insulation tape
7　Spare nylon
8　Blunt nose scissors
9　Artery forceps.
10　Polaroids
11　Priest
12　Wading-Stick
13　Net
14　Insect repellent
15　Fish-carrier
16　Pen knife and string
17　Permit and (England & Wales) rod licence

These items are all that we need for much of our daytime fishing. When fishing in the dark, add:

18　Torch, with spare bulb and batteries

The rest of the tackle can be kept in the tackle-bag in the car or fishing hut until needed:

19　Spare reels and lines
20　Spare flies
21　Lead wire
22　Split-shot or plasticine
23　Wader repair kit
24　Spring balance
25　Thermometer
26　Fish tube
27　Sunblock
28　Band Aid plasters
29　Candle stub
30　Flask and food
31　Spare torch
32　Spare clothing: underclothes, trousers, shirt, sweater, stockings, handkerchief, towel
32　Clothing:Wading jacket
Fishing coat and/or waistcoat
Waterproof over trousers
Neck towel, Mittens
Wader inserts/wader socks
Waders: Breast, thigh, wellies
Hat

FOREWORD
BY HUGH FALKUS

This book is intended as a concise guide to fishing for salmon and sea trout. I have written at length on both subjects in my books *Sea Trout Fishing* and *Salmon Fishing* which, I am happy to say, remain in print. However, not everyone interested in taking up the sport of salmon or sea trout fishing wants to purchase such comprehensive and (unavoidably) expensive books at the outset. Nor do those who like to have a handy reference book with them on fishing trips wish to carry in their baggage the extra weight of the 900 pages of my full length works. Something smaller, more portable and basic in approach, which meets the needs of the beginner and the occasional or holiday angler is called for. In producing this Handbook I have concentrated on the essentials; nonetheless this book contains the distillation of much of what I have learned about fishing for these fascinating migrants during the past 65 years.

Refreshment at sea. HF with Paul Pedersen off the Ravenglass coast.

CONTENTS

ACKNOWLEDGMENTS   5
FOREWORD   7
INTRODUCTION   11

PART ONE
THE ATLANTIC SALMON

CHAPTER 1 INTRODUCING THE SALMON   15
The Anomaly of Salmon Fishing.

CHAPTER 2 FLY-FISHING FOR SALMON   23
Fly-Fishing Tackle, Rod, Reel and Line, Fly Lines, Backing,
Fly Reels, The Fly Rod, Casting, The Leader,
Hooks, Knots, The Wading Stick.

CHAPTER 3 CHOICE AND PRESENTATION OF THE SALMON FLY   38
The Salmon Fly, Presentation, Matters of Depth, Backing-Up,
Dibbling and Riffling, Hooking and Landing a Salmon.

CHAPTER 4 SPINNING   56
Spinning Tackle, Rods, Spoons, Spinners and Plugs,
Swivels and Weights, Fishing Spoons, Spinners and Plugs,
High Water Spinning, Low Water Spinning.

CHAPTER 5 MORE ABOUT THE SPINNER   70
Presentation of the Spinner

CHAPTER 6 WORM FISHING   79
Worm Fishing Tackle, The Worm, Low Water Worming,
High Water Worming, Hooking Fish on Worm.

CHAPTER 7 PRAWN AND SHRIMP FISHING   87
Fishing the Shrimp, The Reactions of a Salmon to the Shrimp,
Tackle for Fishing the Shrimp, Float-Fishing the Shrimp,
Free-Lining a Shrimp.

PART TWO
THE SEA TROUT

CHAPTER 8 INTRODUCING THE SEA TROUT   97
Sea Trout and Salmon Identification, The Life of the Sea Trout,
The Approach to Sea Trout Fishing, Night Fly-Fishing
for Sea Trout.

CHAPTER 9 FLY-FISHING FOR SEA TROUT   110
Tackle Check List, Night Fly-Fishing, Sea Trout Night Flies,
The Sunk Lure, The Surface Lure, Further Notes on Fly Presentation,
Fishing Round the Clock, A Swedish Interlude.

CHAPTER 10 DAYTIME FLY FISHING   137
Fishing a Spate, The Low Water Daytime Wet Fly,
Dry Fly Fishing for Sea Trout, Some Historic Dry Fly
Experiments, Nymph Fishing for Sea Trout.

CHAPTER 11 LAKE FISHING   149
Tackle for Lake Fishing, Lake Flies, Dapping,

CHAPTER 12 SALTWATER FISHING   160
Locating the Fish, Sea Trout Feeding Regime,
Saltwater Fishing Tackle, Flies, Lures and Baits,
Boat Fishing with Fly and Bait.

PART THREE
FISHING WITH FALKUS

CHAPTER 13 SALMON FISHING   183
Tayside in Winter, Five in a Bed.

CHAPTER 14 SEA TROUT FISHING   204
A Night on the River, Sea Trout, Darkness and the Sunk Lure.

CHAPTER 15 TOM RAWLING ON THE FALKUS METHOD   222
Fish all Night for the Big Fish, Sea Trout by the Book.

INTRODUCTION
BY
MALCOLM GREENHALGH

One evening during one of my regular sea trouting trips to Hugh Falkus's beloved River Esk in September 1995 Hugh dragged me into his study. He had not been well for some time. He poured us both a large whisky, bade me sit down, and opened a large cardboard box on his desk.

'I've been trying to get this book written. It's a basic handbook on salmon and sea trout fishing. But I can't write any more. What I have done is all in here. It needs finishing. What I've written needs editing. And there are gaps that need filling. I'd like you to be co-author and get it finished.'

It was with conflicting feelings of deep sorrow, elation and honour that I agreed and, on my return home a couple of days later, I took the box with me. I read through what Hugh had written and then, with trepidation, began work. A week later I returned to Cragg Cottage and slowly took the great man through the editing I had done thus far and some new sections that I had written. Other than correcting some points of grammar, he approved.

Initially this book was intended as a concise summary of what is described at length in Hugh's great textbooks on salmon and sea trout fishing. However, after many subsequent conversations with him, it became our joint decision to adopt a wider brief. Hugh's earlier books are based heavily on his own experience in the British Isles. In the new book I proposed to include descriptions of techniques that are more widely used in other countries, such as dry fly fishing for salmon; and techniques that have only recently been fully developed, such as dry fly and nymph fishing for sea trout and saltwater fishing. We agreed

11

that the book should be as complete as possible, truly a Handbook to complement both Hugh's and my own more lengthy volumes. Hugh christened it the 'Till Book'. His hope was that it would be displayed next to the till in every tackle shop in the world.

I kept Hugh fully informed of the book's development until, in February 1996, he was no longer able to read and edit what I had produced. We last spoke about it on the 12th February when I visited him in hospital.

Hugh Falkus died on 30 March 1996. That day the game angling world lost one whose name will be remembered as long as men and women go fishing for salmon and sea trout; the greatest angler, teacher and writer on the subject that any of us are likely to encounter. I only hope that he would have been as proud of this as he was, rightly, of all his earlier books.

Lowton
April 1997

PART ONE

THE ATLANTIC SALMON

CHAPTER I

INTRODUCING THE SALMON

It is generally agreed that the several species of salmon and trout, both Atlantic and Pacific, came from a common ancestor in the middle of the Miocene Period about 20 million years ago. Whether this ancestor originated in fresh or salt water is uncertain. Biological evidence favours fresh, since most members of the Salmonidae are unable to breed in salt water.

The Atlantic salmon's life cycle starts when the eggs are laid during winter in the gravel bed of some well-oxygenated and fairly fast-flowing stream. An egg takes between three and four months to hatch, and the product - known as an alevin - is a tiny translucent creature with an umbilical sac hanging below its throat.

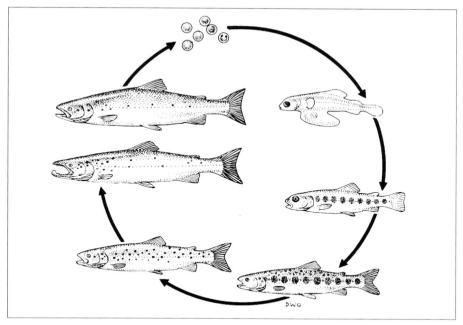

The life cycle of the salmon. (Clockwise from the top) Ova, alevin, fry, parr, smolt, adult.

During the alevin stage the little salmon lives on the contents of its yolk sac, which contains upwards of a month's rations. When the yolk sac has been absorbed the alevin wriggles out of the gravel as a fry.

Now forced to fend for itself, it hunts actively for food, gradually acquiring a form of camouflage in the shape of dark 'finger-marks' along its side. At this stage it is known as a parr and, in general appearance, is very similar to a small brown trout.

Parr feed on fly larvae, tiny crustaceans and other forms of invertebrate life, depending on the food supply available. In turn they are preyed on by a host of enemies. Among many others, kingfishers, herons, mink, otters, cormorants, mergansers, goosanders, pike, perch, chub, eels and other coarse fish have all been known to take their share of immature salmon. The salmon's cousin, the brown trout, is undoubtedly one of its worst enemies. This is not only because of direct predation, but also because the threat of predation impairs the diet selection of young salmon and reduces their rate of feeding. For this reason, the introduction of brown (or rainbow) trout into a salmon river, especially large ones, should never be permitted. Such introduced fish are certain to result in a loss of wild salmon stocks.

When the parr is anything between one and five years old, certain physiological changes take place to fit it for a new environment and then, during May or June, it migrates to sea as a slender, fork-tailed, silvery little fish known as a smolt.

Having reached the river estuary, the salmon smolts encounter further enemies: gulls, terns, shags, pollack, bass, coalfish, congers and many more. But they hurry on towards the rich feeding ground of the open sea. And they go there to grow.

They grow quickly. By the end of their first year at sea they are 20 to 30 times their original weight. Some salmon return to freshwater after just one year at sea; these are called grilse and usually weigh between three and 10lb. Some make their first return to freshwater after a sea life of two, three, and sometimes four years away. But at whatever age they return, return they must, since they cannot spawn in salt water. And on their way back towards their destined rivers they stop feeding.

Recapture of tagged fish indicates that salmon returning from their Atlantic feeding grounds follow quite precise routes. Although a tiny percentage find their way into strange rivers, the majority return to spawn in the rivers of their birth. It is not known exactly how a salmon navigates from the distant ocean to the coast, although recent research suggests that a magnetic indicator in the salmon's head and lateral line is partly responsible, acting as an automatic compass needle. But once the salmon has reached the coast it detects its own parent river by the particular odour of that river. Salmon have an almost unbelievably acute sense of smell.

Having stopped feeding, the returning salmon bring their rations with them and enter the rivers with sufficient reserves in their tissues to sustain them for upwards of 12 months. Not all salmon, of course, endure so long a period of fasting. There is no month of the year in which, in some river, fresh salmon are not running; and whereas those that arrive in winter and spring wait many months before spawning, others spawn only a short time after their late autumn arrival.

It must be noted that some salmon are 'springers' in that they run in spring, some run in summer and some in autumn, and that the autumn and spring runs overlap in some rivers. For instance in November on Tweed it is possible to catch both fresh run autumn and spring fish in one day. Strange, you might think! The autumn fish have well developed ovaries and testes and will spawn only a few weeks after entering the river, in December. By contrast there will be pristine, bright silver salmon with undeveloped ovaries and testes that will remain in the river for another year before spawning. These latter, though they start to run in late autumn and continue to enter the river through the winter (provided water conditions are satisfactory), are referred to as springers because they are the fish that are mostly caught at the beginning of the next season. Angling during the opening few days of the season on several rivers can be excellent simply because of those 'springers' that have accumulated in the river through the winter close season.

Some rivers are famous for their spring fishing (for example, the

Aberdeeenshire Dee, the Cumbrian Eden, Ireland's Drowse) whereas most others receive only a tiny spring run. Many other rivers have excellent summer runs, mainly of grilse, provided water conditions are not too low, and most rivers have an autumn run.

Salmon run upstream according to water temperature, light intensity (movement is slight in bright sunshine and greatest at the 'change of light' around dawn and dusk) and the height of the river. Maximum movement occurs when the water level has fallen (after a rise) to roughly one third of the spate. It is at this time - apart from the first few inches of the rise - that angling chances are at their best.

Extremes of water temperature inhibit salmon migration upriver. Although fish may enter a river at temperatures as low as 34° F, they will not negotiate obstacles and run far upstream until the temperature

Salmon from the river Namsen, Norway. They are 'two sea-winter fish' weighing 14, 17, and 22 lb

is over 40°F. When summer water temperatures rise above 68° F, movement is again inhibited and salmon lie doggo in the deeper pools. Air temperature seems to play no direct part in salmon migration. Provided that light intensity and water levels are congenial, it is water temperature alone that affects their movement.

During the long migration upstream towards the spawning redds, driven on by their ripening sexual urge, salmon force their way past the most formidable obstacles. And what they cannot swim over, they jump. Their leaping has often been exaggerated, but fact is sufficiently dramatic: a perpendicular leap of 11 feet four inches has been measured over the Orrin Falls in Scotland.

By November many of the fish have arrived at their spawning redds. And from then until, usually, about the end of January, most of the spawning takes place.

With the last leaves drifting overhead, the salmon's silver streamlined beauty has vanished. The females are dark, almost black, with bulging bellies; the males reddish brown, huge 'kypes' curving from their lower jaws. After a period of exploratory wandering in shallow, streamy water , the female prepares a spawning bed in the gravel by swimming on her side and flapping with her tail. The male fish, meanwhile, waits in close attendance, ready to drive off all intruders.

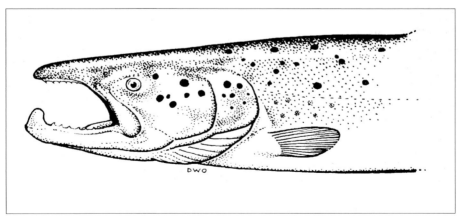

Cock salmon at spawning time with kyped lower jaw.

19

Eventually the female signals her readiness to mate by pressing hard down into the trough she has formed. The male joins her and while he quivers violently beside her, her eggs and his milt are extruded almost simultaneously. Afterwards the male swims away some little distance downstream, whilst the female, by going a yard or so upstream, covers the fertilized eggs with gravel by vigorous flapping movements of her tail.

Two or more sequences may be carried out before the female has deposited all her eggs. Nature prepares for huge losses, each hen fish carrying between 700 and 800 eggs per pound of her body weight.

By the time spawning is finished the fish are emaciated and very weak. These spent fish, or kelts, are little more than two-thirds of their original weight. Their hollow-flanked and ragged-finned bodies are often smothered in fungus; the once oily pink flesh is pale and flaccid. Only comparatively few kelts survive. Of these, most are females.

Male kelt mortality is almost 100% simply because cock salmon lose so much condition during spawning. Female salmon mate only once, twice or three times, until all their eggs have been shed into redds. By contrast cock salmon will, given the chance, spawn with several hens and waste a great deal of energy attempting to mate with hen kelts (who ignore such approaches) and even with inanimate objects such as boulders and stranded logs.

Those kelts that regain the rich feeding grounds of the sea recover their condition very quickly. Strangely, those that return to freshwater for a second spawning have a fat content as high as or, in some cases, even higher than that of virgin fish.

The proportion of salmon that survive a third spawning is very small indeed. Only the exceptional fish returns to spawn a fourth time.

It is significant that surviving kelts don't leave the river together when seemingly able to do so, but over a period that may extend into several months. Here again, as with the staggered arrival of incoming fish, Nature tries to insure against the possibility of total loss.

The Anomaly of Salmon Fishing

When we think of it, the catching of a salmon on rod and line seems highly improbable, whether with natural bait or an artificial lure such as a 'fly' or spinner. After all, why on earth should anyone expect to hook a fish that has no appetite? But that in effect is the problem confronting every salmon angler, for what he is trying to do is to catch a fish that is not hungry; that while waiting in the river to spawn, lives on the fat stored in its tissues and has no need of food. It makes little or no effort to search for food, being content to lie where it is in a congenial resting-place where it can enjoy some well-oxygenated water. In consequence of this, the angler usually finds the salmon a very difficult fish to catch. Indeed, what seems remarkable is that he catches one at all. Often, of course, he doesn't!

Nevertheless, he will catch one sooner or later, if he persists, because, surprisingly, there are times when salmon will react to and take a variety of baits or lures, sometimes quite avidly.

Nobody knows why salmon behave in this unexpected manner. We must be content with theory. And from a large number of theories that have been propounded, the most plausible is that salmon take from habit or from aggression. Habit: the feeding habit formed during its life at sea and, perhaps, during its earlier river life as a parr. Aggression: the desire to kill or snap at something that has invaded its resting lie. Yet the remarkable point remains that, for many hours, a salmon may see anglers' flies passing overhead and then, suddenly, take. And what is even more remarkable is that, in one river on one day, several salmon may take within the space of a few minutes, and on a variety of lures and baits, yet not a single fish will be taken through the remaining hours of the day. Why such 'magic moments'? Why such distinct, short-lived 'taking times'? Surely the feeding habit or aggressive traits would be there all day long; not be awakened for just a few moments.

Whatever the reasons may be for salmon to take the bait or lure, the experienced angler has learned that a salmon's reaction to any sort of lure is based mainly on the prevailing temperature and the height of the water. It is on these that the choice of lure size and method of fishing will depend. The experienced hand knows that in early spring he may fail to catch because his lure is too small, and in summer he may fail because it is too big. When the water temperature is low - as it is in early spring and late autumn - he will fish a quick-sinking fly line or heavily weighted spinning rig and a large lure, two to four inches long. Perhaps even longer. And when the water temperature rises with warmer weather into the high 40°s F, he will change to a small lure an inch or so in length, sometimes much less, fished close to the surface. Indeed, if the air temperature is much higher than the water temperature, he may change tactics to the small lure fished close to the surface when the water temperature is still in the range 45°-48° F. This rough guide to lure size and depth at which the lure is fished comes from angling experience.

As such, it is a guide that will help the novice to catch fish. It is true that there is a large element of luck in salmon fishing. There are no certainties. If he persists the beginner is always in with a chance. Yet the veteran angler will catch more fish in the long run simply because in addition to his ration of luck he has the knowledge born of experience. A beginner should take every possible opportunity of fishing for salmon to gain his own experience.

CHAPTER 2

FLY-FISHING FOR SALMON

Fly Fishing Tackle

When it comes to purchasing fishing tackle, buy the best you can afford. There is more to fishing than catching fish, and the pleasure that comes from using good quality tackle is an important part of it. Sooner or later, cheap stuff will let you down. All too many anglers have fallen for 'bargain' offers, and found themselves at the waterside, far from home, with a rod that has shattered, a line that will not cast properly, and a broken reel. Very expensive, such bargains!

Rod, Reel and Line

The first purchases made by someone who decides to take up salmon fishing are always rod, reel and line; usually in that order. It is essential, however, to consider these three separate items as one single purchase with three components, for they must work together in harmony. The reason for this is the fact that flyrods and lines are matched together in what is known as the AFTM system*

Fly-Lines

The fly-line must be considered first, for it is the weight of the line that makes the rod flex to propel the fly out across the water.

Fly-lines are rated (according to their weight) in the AFTM system, AFTM #1 being the lightest and #12 the heaviest (actually there are even heavier lines for saltwater fly fishing). An AFTM #1 will cast the lightest of trout dry flies in windless conditions, but not a heavy salmon fly, nor any fly in blustery conditions.

The AFTM line classification system includes two other components:
1. The line profile or taper

---

* AFTM: a system of classifying fly lines and their matching rods by the Association of Fishing Tackle Manufacturers.

Floating fly line. No 7 Double Taper.

Sink Tip No 7 fly line. Weight Forward.

Sinking No 7 fly line. Weight Forward.

Intermediate or slow sinking No 7 fly line. Weight Forward.

Fly lines from Cortland, U. S. A. The line containers are labelled to show the type, AFTM no. and length of each line. 'Rocket Taper' is the term Cortland use to describe their Weight Forward lines

    + DT = double taper (essential for all roll- or Speycasting)
    + WF = weight forward (the profile for long distance, over-
head casting); sometimes called 'rocket taper' lines
    + SH = shooting head (a line for long distance overhead casting.)
 2. Line types
    + F = Floating (the entire line floats)
    + I = Intermediate (a very slow sinking line)
    + S = Sinking (the line sinks.There are lines with different sink-
ing rates, e.g. Wet Cel I and Wet Cel II, or Slow Sink, Medium Sink,
Fast Sink)
    +FS = Sink Tip (most of the line floats, though the tip section
sinks). This information is marked on the box in which the fly line is
sold. Thus a line marked DT11F is a double-tapered No. 11 floater.
    The aim of the floating line is to hold the fly close to the surface
(dry fly, on the surface), and of the sinking line to take the fly deep.
The sink tip is useful in fast water where the floating line may cause
the fly to skate across the surface. Because of the difficulty of obtaining a well designed sink tip (Scientific Anglers produce the best one
we could find), many anglers prefer the intermediate line, a very slow
sinker that, in turbulent fast flows, fishes the fly at the desired depth.
    The following lines are essential for salmon (and sea trout) river
fishing:

        For the 12-15' carbon double-handed rods: DT10-12F,
DT10-12FS, DT10-12I, DT10-12S, the actual number to be matched
with the rod. DT because we will be Spey-casting.
        For the 10'6" carbon single-handed salmon and sea trout
        rod: DT7F, DT7FS, DT7I, DT7S.

    AFTM7 is the perfect weight of line to cast the wide range of
salmon and sea trout flies that will be used with the single-handed rod.
For roll-casting and Spey-casting choose the DT line. For long distance overhead casting a WF line is preferable.

Backing-Line
Backing is a reserve of line available for playing a lively fish. It is advisable to have at least 150 yards on your reel, for when you need backing (when a big fish takes off) you need it badly. Braided nylon or nylon monofilament makes good backing, being rot-proof, strong and thin. About 30lb test. How to attach fly-line and backing to a reel is described below.

Fly-Reels
A fly-reel is simply a revolving drum big enough to hold the fly line and backing; but, as we soon appreciate when a big salmon sets off at speed, only the best reel is good enough. Avoid cheap reels. Sooner or later they will let you down and cause the loss of a fish. In simple terms of cash value, that fish will probably outweigh the cost of a good reel.

All good reels have an efficient check- or drag-adjuster. Set this so that, when you pull off line quickly (as when a fish makes a sudden dash) the reel does not over-run; yet not so tightly that the fish needs to jerk hard to pull off line. Too tight a reel-check and, instead of the reel giving line, the hook hold may be pulled out instead.

FITTING FLY-LINE AND BACKING ONTO A REEL

a. Take reel, line and backing to a field.
b. Tie the end of the fly-line onto the reel first (use a fine piece of thread).
Note: in a DT line you can use either end, but if one end of the fly line carries a tag saying 'This End' or 'Reel', that end must be attached to the backing, so begin by attaching the other end (without the tag) to the empty reel.
c. Wind the fly-line onto the reel and then attach the end of the backing using loop connection (p 33).
d. Now wind backing onto the reel until the reel is full.
e. Pull all the backing and fly-line off the reel as you walk across the field.
f. Attach the end of the backing to the now-empty reel using the Reel Knot (p 32). Make sure that this knot is 100% tight.
g. Wind on backing and fly-line.
You now have a full reel, with fly-line on top, ready for action

The following reels are essential:
>For AFTM10-12 lines plus at least 150 yards of backing:
>>4" diameter, wide-spool reels
>For AFTM7 lines plus at least 100 yards of backing:
>>3½" wide - or 3½" narrow-spool reels

The Fly-Rod

Irrespective of its construction the salmon fly-rod - like any other fly-rod a spring when we are casting a line and a lever when we are playing a fish - is simply an extension of our arms. Its chief function is to help us cast the fly-line to present the fly. Second in importance, since it is longer than our arms, is the help it gives us in keeping the line clear of the water and so free from obstructions and the drag of the current while a fish is being played. Any relationship between a rod's size and strength and the size of the salmon it lands is coincidental. Indeed, provided our reserve of line is adequate, and the leader is of suitable breaking-strain, the biggest salmon can be landed on the smallest rod. A singlehanded rod may be adequate for summer fishing on small rivers with very small flies; but it is inadequate for fishing a big river, or a big, heavy lure in spring. The reason for using such long double-handed rods is convenience. The longer and stronger the rod, the more easily can a long line be cast in one action, without false-casting; the more efficiently can the fly be controlled when we are fishing it across the river; the long rod gives us a better command of the fish when we are playing him.

What dictates the choice of rod is not the size of the fish; it is the method of fishing, the type of lure and line, and the distance that has to be cast (which is a function of the size of the river), bearing in mind that the object is to do so as easily as possible.

It is on the accurate placing of the line, which presents our fly where it may attract a fish, that successful salmon flyfishing depends. As a general principle, wherever you are fishing, use a rod of sensible length, but do not imagine that any one salmon rod will cope with all fishing situations. It won't. Anyone who aims to fish a wide variety of salmon rivers throughout the season needs more than one rod.

+15' carbon taking AFTM 11-12 lines: big rivers (such as Spey, Tweed, Tay) throughout the season; also medium sized rivers in spring and late autumn, when sunk line fishing with big tube flies.

+12'-14' carbon taking AFTM 10 line: small rivers and medium rivers in summer and autumn, when fishing floating lines with small flies.

+10' 6" carbon (single-handed) taking AFTM 7 lines: small rivers; medium rivers in high summer, low water conditions; where the fly has to be worked.

+11'-12' carbon (single-handed) taking AFTM 6-7 lines: loch fishing for salmon or sea trout.

*Carbon fibre rods are excellent conductors of electricity. Beware of overhead power lines!

Fly rods are marked with their length and the appropriate weight of line (AFTM) above the handle.

Choosing a rod

Never buy a rod without testing it first. All good retailers will allow you to try out a rod. The manufacturers' stands at the Game Fair or the Chatsworth Angling Fair provide ample scope for trials before purchase. Never buy a rod by mail order without having had a few casts with it first. Many have done so, and regretted it.

The Flash Problem

Most fishing rods are sold with a gloss varnish finish and, often, with shiny fittings. These flash in the sun and warn the fish of the approaching angler. Revarnish all flashy rods with a matt varnish.

Cover up or remove your wrist watch before starting to fish. In sunny conditions it acts as a small heliograph, announcing your presence by flashing downstream into the fishes' eyes.

"Highly-varnished rods with bright fittings are very objectionable. The more quiet and sober are the colours of the angler's rod, dress, and impedimenta generally, the more fish he is likely to catch."

(John Bickerdyke, 1888.)

As HF was fond of pointing out, nothing much in advice to anglers is new.

Care of rods, reels and fly-lines

- Always transport rods from home to river in rigid rod tubes.

- Check rods regularly for broken or bent rod rings, frayed whippings etc.

- A common cause of rod breakage is separation of the joints during casting (especially Spey-casting). Lightly wax spigots (this also prevents wear); tape joints securely with electrician's insulation tape .

- Store reels, when not in use, in padded reel bags or boxes.

(If the rod does not have a screw-tight reel-seat and instead uses sliding rings, tape the reel-seat to prevent the reel falling off. There is nothing worse than playing a salmon with the reel lying in three feet of fast water!)

- Special creams are available for treating fly lines: these will pro-

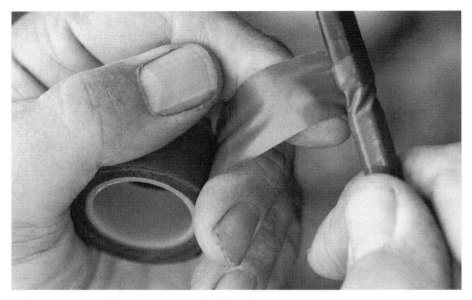

Always tape rod joints, especially when Spey-casting

long the life of your lines and also keep the lines supple. Never tread on fly lines or let them come into contact with organic solvents. The life of a fly line can also be extended by keeping it in a polythene bag in the cool and dark during long periods when you are not fishing.

Good fishing tackle is expensive, and popular with thieves. It is also easy to break a rod accidentally. Insure all your fishing tackle against theft and accidental breakage during storage at home, when in transit to and from the river, and when in use.

Casting

The wrong time to learn to cast is when you go fishing. Learn beforehand and, during spells without fishing, spend a few hours each week practising.

Learn to Spey-cast. Spey-casting removes the need to false-cast. False-casting is a habit that wastes time and effort, and, with the line flashing to and fro over the fish, causes disturbance.

Speycasting
- is safer than overhead casting, for the fly never passes behind you.
- cannot result in damage to the hook, when the fly on the backcast hits a stone on the bank.
- is less tiring than overhead casting.
- is a delightful exercise in its own right.

There is not space here to describe the roll, single-Spey and double-Spey casts. They are described in HF's book *Speycasting* (1994). Money spent on a few lessons with a good instructor is not wasted.

The Leader

The leader is simply a slender nylon link between fly-line and fly. There is no need to err on the side of lightness. The first responsibility of any angling sportsman is to avoid being broken; and salmon show no signs of being unduly 'gut-shy'. It is both sensible and sporting to use the strongest link compatible with the size of fly we happen to be using.

Tapered leaders are available but unnecessary. Although it is true that a tapered leader will turn over slightly better at the completion of a cast, a length of level nylon will serve perfectly well in most instances (exceptions are dry fly fishing for sea trout, and lake fishing with a team of wet flies. Tapered leaders can be made up by joining several nylon lengths using a Water Knot (see *Knots* on p 32).

A time when we need to taper the leader is when we change down in size of fly. A small fly will not 'work' attractively on nylon that is too thick. So, when going from, say, a size 8 to a size 12 fly, we may change our leader-point in sympathy.

A useful tip: Buy all monofilament from a big retail outlet where turnover is rapid. Then you can be sure that the stuff has not been in store for ages and already deteriorated. After 12 months, replace all spools of monofil (certainly of 10lb B.S. or less).

Care of nylon: Nylon loses its strength and elasticity, and becomes more brittle, when exposed to sunlight or high temperatures. Store spools in the dark and cool.

Hooks

For salmon flies, double and treble hooks have the edge over singles, up to size 6*. For larger flies, tubes, with a small treble at the rear, are better, though a large single is considered by some anglers to be the most effective hook for landing very big fish. By contrast, big doubles and trebles are least effective at hooking fish.

*For most salmon hooks (in the size range 2-16), the bigger the number the smaller the hook size.

There are several brands of good quality salmon hooks available. Partridge (now owned by the Norwegian manufacturer Mustad) produces an excellent range. The Japanese have entered the market with some high quality products. Beware their 'chemically sharpened' hooks. These are becoming more popular. Though superb for bait fishing, for trout and salmon fishing these hooks are too sharp! Furthermore, the nature of chemical sharpening makes it impossible to re-sharpen or take away some of the stickiness from such hooks. To attempt to do so ruins the hook point. So avoid hooks that are chemically sharpened.

Knots

Important: when completing any knot tied in nylon fishing line:

Always lubricate the knot with saliva before pulling tight

Always, when pulling the knot tight, do it very slowly and check that each turn slides snugly into place.

Remember that the knot is always the weakest link between you and the fish and that, if there is a breakage, on 99% of occasions it will be the knot that gives.

Reel Knot

For tying backing to reel drum. Note the stop-knot that prevents slippage.

Fly-line Loop Knot

An excellent way of fixing backing to fly-line, and leader butt to fly-line, is by Loop-to-Loop (see diagram). In order to achieve this you need to tie loops at both ends of the fly-line.

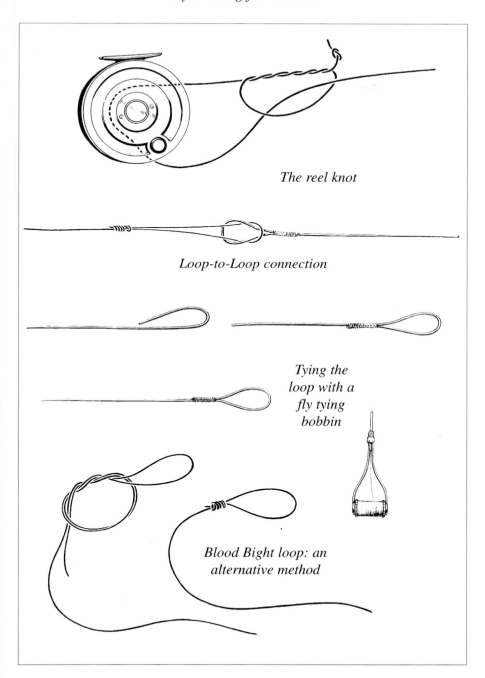

The reel knot

Loop-to-Loop connection

Tying the
loop with a
fly tying
bobbin

Blood Bight loop: an
alternative method

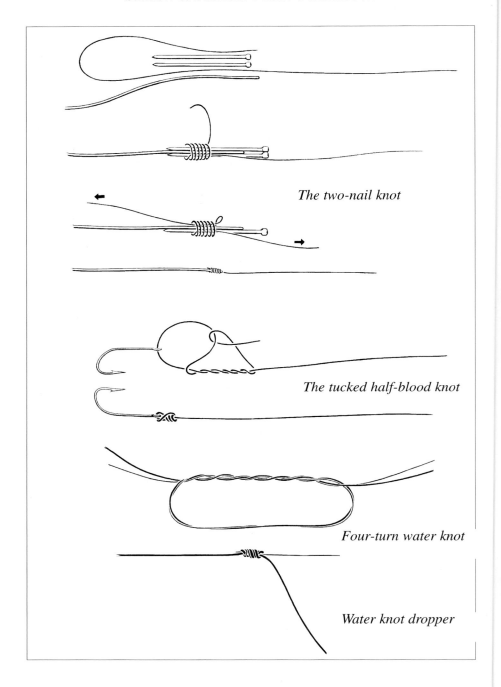

The two-nail knot

The tucked half-blood knot

Four-turn water knot

Water knot dropper

Make a loop in the end of the fly-line.

Using strong thread, whip the base of the loop tightly. The best and easiest way to do this is with a thread bobbin in a fly-tying bobbin-holder which provides the necessary weight for you to wrap thread round the loop base by swinging the bobbin round and round, tightly. You can 'brake' the bobbin by taking one or two turns of the thread round one of the legs of the bobbin.

Whip-finish and give the thread whippings at least three coats of varnish, allowing drying time between coats.

Knot dimensions: the final loop needs to be about half an inch long, with the securing whipped portion also about half an inch long.

Blood Bight Loop The knot to use when a loop is needed in the end of a piece of nylon (or fine Dacron backing). For setting up a fly-fishing rig, tie Blood Bight Loops in the end of the backing (here a loop should be large enough to allow the reel to pass through: 6 inches long); in the leader butt.

Double the line and make three turns as shown. Wet and pull tight slowly.

Loop-to-Loop Connections

The ideal way of linking backing to fly-line and fly-line to leader butt. Some anglers worry at first about having such apparently big knots (a large Blood Bight Loop Knot in the backing attached to a Fly-line Loop Knot in the fly-line.) Will it slip through the rod-rings when a big fish surges off downstream? Yes. It most certainly will! It also allows fly-lines to be changed on one reel easily. Coil the fly-line and release the Loop-to-Loop Connection; fix on the new coiled fly-line with another Loop-to-Loop Connection and then wind it on the reel.

Two Nail Knot

An alternative method for tying a nylon leader butt to the fly-line. Always have a couple of nails in the fishing bag.

Arrange two nails (it is easier with two than the traditional one), the end of the fly-line and a loop in the end of the leader, as shown.

Make six full turns with the end of the nylon around fly-line and the nails, as shown.

Use of the wading stick

Slide out one of the nails (the other provides a stiffener for completing the knot). Pass the end of the nylon through the knot, using the gap left when the nail was removed, as shown. Remove the second nail, wet the knot and slowly pull tight.

Tucked Blood Knot
The most popular and very secure knot for tying hooks, flies, swivels, spinners etc. to nylon line.

Slip the end of the nylon through the eye and make four full turns; then pass end of line through the loop formed by first turn immediately in front of the eye (the 'tuck'), as shown. Wet and pull tight.

Four-turn Water Knot The easiest way of tying together two lengths of nylon, and the most straightforward way of tying in droppers.

Align the two ends, allowing plenty of overlap for tying the knot, create a big loop with the two lines and make four turns, as shown.

Wet and slowly pull the knot tight before trimming away the two waste ends.

If making a tapered leader with a dropper attached, retain the forward pointing 'waste' end (ie the length that points towards the end of the leader). Some writers have suggested that the other, rear-pointing 'waste' end be used because it sticks out better from the leader and will hold the dropper fly away from the leader. We do not recommend this. Tie your dropper fly to that end and a big fish may break the knot. In practice, the fly is held as well in the water on the forward pointing end as on the rear pointing end.

The Wading Stick

A wading-stick is the most important item of subsidiary tackle. Sooner or later it will save the angler from a ducking. It may even save his life. But there are wading-sticks and wading-sticks!

A good wading-stick forms a strut, heavy enough at the base to stand beside you, even in a strong flow, ready-to-hand. It should be tipped with rubber to reduce underwater noise, and slung so that the handle is always within reach. Its length should be such that, with the end on the bottom, the handle is well out of the water when you are wading waist deep - otherwise your hand goes under and you get a wet sleeve. Very cold in early spring. A good wading-stick should also have a lanyard attachment that is easy to unclip (as, for example, when you have come ashore to play a fish and the wading-stick becomes an encumbrance). For added security, use a rubber band as 'preventer', to prevent the lanyard becoming unclipped.

Salmon Fly Fishing Check List

See inside front cover.

CHAPTER 3

CHOICE AND PRESENTATION
OF THE SALMON FLY

The Salmon Fly

It is well worth tying your own salmon flies. Fly tying is an enjoyable hobby in itself which provides diversion during the dark winter months. Obtaining hooks and materials is part of the fun of tying your own flies. There is no need to seek out the exotic plumage and complicated recipes of our forefathers. Some dyed squirrel tails, a few feathers and a twist of silver or gold tinsel will furnish any number of killing salmon flies. All you need to learn is the basic tying technique. One of the best simple methods is that described by Arthur Oglesby, a long-standing friend of HF and a famous salmon catcher. Here it is, reproduced with Arthur's kind permission from his book *Salmon:*

"For small flies I rely on the most simple dressing. The selected hook [a Partridge double salmon hook, size 8, for example] is placed in a vice and the shank covered lightly with clear Bostik. A few turns of binding silk are then spun onto the shank and wound down to the point where the body will finish. A length of fine tinsel wire is then bound in, followed by a split length of marabou silk. The tying silk is then taken to the head of the fly, and the body silk is bound round the shank until it is locked into position at the head. Following this, the tinsel is wound round in open spirals until it too is tied in position at the head of the fly. It is fairly important to bind in the tinsel in a different direction to that taken by the body silk, so that it helps to keep the silk bound in if a fish should cut the silk at any time. A few hackle fibres are then taken from a suitable feather and bound in underneath the eye of the hook. All that is then left to do is to select some squirrel or bucktail winging of suitable colour and tie this on top of the shank. The whole is then bound in with tying silk and a further addition of clear Bostik. A final whip knot completes the dressing and the knot is lacquered with black enamel to give a professional finish to the head.

Big flies on tubes are even more simple to dress. I now rarely bother with any body materials, but tie in the various colours of bucktail winging and finish off as before. I am not a great advocate of having the fibres extending much further than the hook position, since there is a possibility that the fish might nip the end of the fly without coming into contact with the hook.

On most of my big flies I like plenty of dressing; but on the very small ones it is sometimes difficult to keep the dressing sufficiently sparse. I am not greatly concerned with pattern, but I do like to have a wide variety of sizes, with further variables on the amount of dressing those sizes contain. I suggest a bit of experimentation, even if you are ashamed to show your flies to more talented fly-dressing friends. The only yardstick by which they should be judged is whether they catch fish!"

In this illogical sport of salmon fishing, which consists of offering a meal to fish that are not hungry, it is obviously important for the angler to bolster his confidence, for only if he is confident in what he is doing will he persist, and persistence is essential. But what confidence can anyone have in any fly and method of presenting it if fly and method have not been chosen for some particular reason, be it fact or fancy?

Many theories have been advanced concerning colours and patterns of salmon flies. Much debate has surrounded the appropriate choice of fly for particular conditions of light. It is probable, in spite of the pundits, that if you select any one pattern of fly that for whatever reason gives you confidence, and fish it in varying sizes and degrees of dressing throughout the season, you will do as well as you would had you a host of patterns to choose from. Indeed, you are likely to do better, since you will not waste time debating what pattern to use.

The most important point to consider when choosing a fly is the size. The following table summarises fly sizes according to different water temperatures:

Water Temperature °F (°C)	Fly Size
Less than 42° (6°)	2-4" tube
42-50° (°6-10°)	hook size 2-6 or 1-1$\frac{1}{2}$" tube
50-55° (10-12.5°)	hook size 6-8 or $\frac{3}{4}$"-1" tube
55-60° (12.5-15°)	hook size 8-10 or $\frac{1}{2}$"- $\frac{3}{4}$" tube
60-65° (15-17.5°) or $\frac{1}{4}$-$\frac{1}{2}$" tube	hook size 10-12
above 65° (17.5°)	hook size 12-16

Treble hook sizes to match tubes

Tube length	Treble hook size
up to $\frac{1}{2}$"	10-14
$\frac{1}{2}$"-1"	8-10
1"-2"	6-8
2"-3"	4-6
4"	4

These figures provide a rough guide. If the water temperature is at the lower end of the range, start with a larger fly and be prepared to go smaller. In high water use a bigger fly. Low water, small fly. In coloured water use a bigger fly than when the river is running clear.

In faster, more turbulent water, as in pool necks and sometimes in the tails, use a fly one size larger than in smoother, more evenly flowing water.

Choosing a Fly

An important point to consider when choosing a fly is the amount of dressing on the hook. A slender lightly dressed fly will sink faster than a bushy one tied on a similar hook. And since small hooks weigh less than bigger ones, a lightly dressed size 8 may fish at the same depth as, say, a bushy size 6 on the same length of leader, given the same fly line and the same water flow. The amount of dressing on the fly has a crucial bearing on how that fly will fish. It is worth remembering the sage advice of the late T.R.Henn, Cambridge don and a superb flydresser: "When making coffee, use twice as much as you think you need; when tying flies, use half as much."

Notes on Fly patterns

Stoat's tails are black hair-winged flies; real stoat being hard to come by, the wing of such flies nowadays is usually made of dyed squirrel tail or bucktail. Any durable black hair will do. A famously successful Spey gillie we know swears by dyed skunk tail as the ideal wing for salmon flies. Black hair-wing flies are as good as any for salmon and make an excellent first choice.

The Willie Gunn is a champion, with its mixed hair wing of black, orange and yellow. It succeeds in all sizes. Some salmon fishers use no other fly, but vary the dressing according to the water conditions. In clearer water they use more black, and in coloured water more orange.

The Yellow (or Garry) Dog, named after a dog who provided the hair, is a useful 'first change' to tie on when spirits are flagging. Ted Browne, a friend of MG from Northern Ireland, fishes only this fly. In 1994 he caught 84 salmon and in the following year 76 salmon on it. Ted has confidence in the Yellow Dog and instead of worrying about different patterns, concentrates on size and presentation.

Shrimp patterns are rightly popular, especially in peaty or falling

Light dressing

Heavy dressing

Even though to our eyes, the lightly dressed fly may seem so sparsely dressed that the fish will find it difficult to see, light dressings are often far more effective than heavy dressings.

waters and in autumn. Ally's Shrimp (by Alastair Gowan) is one of the best.

Presentation of the Fly
The three key points:
1. Is the fly fishing at the correct depth?
2. Is the fly fishing at the correct speed?
3. Is the fly fishing at the best angle to achieve correct depth and speed?

Matters of Depth
In late winter and early spring, and again on some rivers in late autumn when water temperatures are below 45°F, the fly is best fished deep. From mid spring, usually about the end of April but in very cold springs as late as mid May, when water temperatures have risen above 50°F, the fly is best fished close to the surface. There is then a transition period (water temperature between 45° and 50° F) when a deeply

A selection of salmon flies: **Top** *Willie Gunn.* **Second row** *Stoat's Tail and Yellow Dog.* **Third row** *Silver Stoat's Tail and Ally's Shrimp.* **Bottom** *MG's Arctic Fox Shrimp.*

fished big fly or a smaller fly fished just below the surface might equally attract the salmon. Air temperature has some effect during this period. When the air is warmer than the water the small fly fished close to the surface is always in with a chance, even with water temperature as low as 42°-44° F. When the air is appreciably colder than the water, the big fly fished deep will take fish even with water temperature at 52°-54°F. As a general rule, however, the small fly fished close to the surface is effective from mid April to late autumn.

In order to explain the reaction of salmon to the angler's lure at different water temperatures we need to consider the physiology of the fish. Being a cold-blooded (poikilothermal) creature, the salmon's body temperature is approximately that of the river water in which it swims. Energy production in the body depends on body temperature which in turn depends on water temperature. Thus the colder the water, the more lethargic the fish. Hence the well-known fact that salmon are unable or unwilling to ascend low waterfalls and whitewater rapids in water temperature below about 42°F. They have insufficient energy to do so. And the bigger the waterfall, the more energy they need to ascend.

This water temperature/energy level relationship affects many aspects of salmon behaviour in fresh water. In cold water not only is the fish's energy level reduced but its vision mechanism – eye, optic nerve, brain – operates much slower than when the water is warmer. Salmon fishing in cold water therefore requires appropriate tactics to take these factors into account, ie the use of a big fly fished deep, slow and close to the fish. Conversely, when the water temperature has risen, the salmon is lively and may seize a tiny fly fished more rapidly and passing above its head, close to the surface.

From the above, the novice will realise that possession of a thermometer is very desirable. And since salmon fishing is by no means an exact science, equally desirable is the possession of two rods equipped with floating and sinking lines in order to have alternative tactics readily available in case the salmon decides to do the opposite of that which the above theory may lead the angler to expect.

For warm water summer fishing where the ideal depth for fishing the fly is roughly four to six inches below the surface, it is customary to fish with a floating line. This is fine for shallow, bouldery, streamy water up to four feet deep. However, in more turbulent, fast, deep water the Intermediate (very slow sinking) line or the sink tip are often more effective. In big fast rivers like the Spey or some Norwegian waters, where the weight of current tends to push the line high, it may be necessary to fish a medium sinking line with the small fly.

For cold water conditions in early spring or late autumn a sinking line is essential. In shallow or slow pools a medium sinker may do, but on most waters a fast sinker will be required and on some deep burly rivers like the lower Tweed, Tay and Spey, even an ultra fast sinker.

Fly Weight and Type

For summer salmon fishing, our preference is for double and treble hooks in sizes from 14 (small) to 6 (medium). For larger sizes the tube is the best bet.

For cold water sunk line conditions the tube is essential. Tubes come in three weights: light plastic, medium heavy aluminium and heavy brass. In 95% of rivers and in most conditions the aluminium tube has the edge over the brass. Fished on a fly line dense enough to get deep, the aluminium tube swims nicely off the bottom and is much easier to cast. On balance it is better to choose a heavy line and slightly lighter fly to gain necessary depth rather than a moderately heavy line and a very heavy tube.

The heavy brass tube comes into its own when you are fishing deep water from a boat or fishing turbulent deep water either wading or from the bank. On a big river when the water is fining down after a spate the salmon will rest in deep slack water usually close to the bank, off the main current. Assuming these fish to be under your bank, the brass tube is cast down and across into the main flow, an upstream mend is made and by the time the lure has reached the slacker water it will have sunk to the correct fishing depth.

Whatever type of fly line is used, the depth the fly fishes and the speed it fishes can to some extent be controlled by varying the angle of the cast and by varying the amount of slack line on or in the water. Slack line may be used to slow down a fly's passage through the water by the process called 'mending' the line. After the cast is made, the angler throws a loop of line upstream against the current to reduce drag. A similarly effective tactic is to move downstream five paces immediately after the cast is made, in order to slow the line speed and increase the fly's fishing depth. Both these ploys are easier to do than to describe.

The experienced salmon fisher varies tactics according to the water

Five different styles of salmon lure: Waddington Willie Gunn (a), Collie Dog tube (b), Prawn Fly double (c), Stoat's Tail treble (d), and Marabou hairwing dressed on a single hook (e).

With rod held high the angler varies the amount of slack line on the water

current. In slack water he will cast square across and strip in line to give movement to the fly; in a sluggish current he will cast a longer line at a slightly more acute angle, allowing a belly to form in the line which will swing the fly over the lies at the correct speed and depth; in a medium current the cast will be made at a more acute angle still on an even longer line. In summer, using a floating or sink tip line, the line is mended as soon as a belly has formed. In cold water conditions, using the sinking line, the mend is made immediately after casting. In a fast current the cast will be made from a position further upstream of the lie, requiring a long throw and an immediate mend and also the shooting of an extra yard or two of line as well.

Note: Mending should only be practised in broken or rippled water where it is unlikely to cause disturbance. On smooth surfaces like low water summer pools, it will do more harm than good.

Apart from knowledge of the water, it is the ability to ring the changes by juggling fly weight, line density and fishing technique that

In slow water the fly's speed can be accelerated by allowing a belly to form in the line

Fast water. The fly can be slowed to some extent by wading and reducing the angle of the cast

distinguishes the successful salmon fisher. Although there is a considerable element of luck in salmon fishing, some anglers catch more than others. Their success is not entirely due to good luck – it derives from attention to detail.

Three Minor Tactics: Backing up, Dibbling and Riffling

The experienced salmon angler always has a few tricks in his repertoire (we will abandon the his or her; women fishers are included in all our definitions.) Here are three that can bring results on a dour day:

Backing Up

If you have the pool to yourself, backing up will sometimes catch fish that might not otherwise be caught.

Backing up has virtues apart from the conventional downstream method. It is effective in slow still pools where the current is too slack to work the fly (for example, on the Thurso, which glides slowly over an almost level gradient with few of the streamy riffles and pools of the majority of salmon rivers).

Fishing the conventional method, the angler works slowly downstream taking a pace or two between casts. This way, the fish must see the fly coming ever closer, a yard or so at a time, and each time from one direction. But when backing up, where the angler starts fishing at the lower end of the pool and progresses upstream, the fly appears suddenly in the salmon's view, from a different direction, and will sometimes provoke a 'crunch' take.

THE SUCCESSFUL ANGLER ACHIEVES HIS (OR HER) RESULTS BY:

1. Using water sense and intuition (ability to read the water)
2. Stealth. Concealment. Avoidance of causing shadow or vibration by clumsy approach to the waterside.
3. Using well balanced tackle suitable for the water
4. Correct choice and presentation of the fly
5. Ability to wade deep and stealthily
6. Ability to cast accurately and where necessary to cast a long line and to control it effectively (this includes the ability to Spey cast).

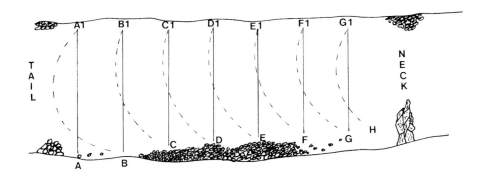

The angler starts at the pool tail and works upstream. From position A he casts to A1 and then, with the rod held low over the water, slowly moves upstream to B. The next cast is to B1, the angler moving upstream to C and so on.

When backing up it is imperative to keep well back from the lies and to cast with extra care. Fishing this way, you may be wading alongside fish that you will be trying to catch on your next cast. Move with extreme caution. Don't frighten the fish. Keep out of sight as far as possible.

Dibbling and Riffling

These are techniques which keep the fly working or skating in the water surface, something that we try to avoid when fishing the conventional way. As with backing up, dibbling and riffling are commonly practised on some rivers (in northern Scotland, for example) but completely neglected on others. They can nonetheless be applied on all salmon rivers as useful and amusing subsidiary tactics.

Dibbling is used in fast, turbulent water where the salmon lie is close to the angler's position (say about one 15 ft rod's length distant). Ideally, the angler should be on the bank and above the lie. A stealthy approach is necessary.

A two-fly cast is used. The leader, of 10-15lb nylon, 10 ft long, carries a wet fly, such as a small double, on the point and four feet up the

Backing-up a long pool the angler is hand-lining to keep the fly moving.

cast, a bushy dropper or something like a Yellow Dolly, developed by Derek Knowles for this method of fishing (see his *Salmon on a Dry Fly*).This is cast across the lie and held on a tight line so that the dropper works across the surface. The fly is kept stationary, then allowed to drift downstream, then checked and tweaked across, then manoeuvred upstream, in a series of enticing movements designed to provoke the salmon into seizing the fly. Dibbling calls for concentration. Nothing may happen for a while, then suddenly a fish will snatch the fly. It is all too easy to be startled into striking, which is fatal. Let the fish have the fly and turn down before you set the hook.

Riffling is another technique where the fly is skated across the surface which is used in water with a steadier, less turbulent flow and with conventional casts. There are two ways of making a fly riffle: first, with a fly tied on a regular salmon hook, tie the fly to the end of the leader and then tie a 'Portland Hitch' behind the head (see illustration). The fly will fish being pulled from the side as it swims down and across the river, and it will skate or riffle through the surface. The second way uses plastic tubes. Make a hole about a quarter of the way

51

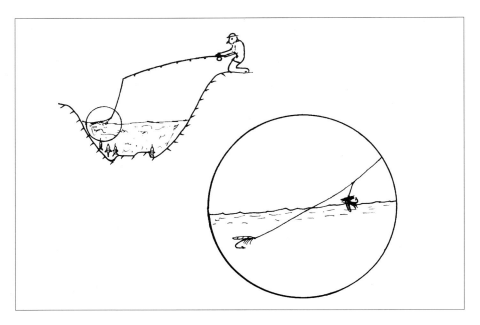

Although it is said that Dibbling is a technique that works only to the north of the Great Glen, it will work anywhere provided that the fish are lying in streamy water within five or six yards of the bank, and that the angler can approach and present the fly without disturbing the fish.
The flies are lowered onto the water (not 'cast'), with the minimum length of fly-line beyond the rod tip. The flies are bounced on the water, and pulled across the front of the fish, then allowed to drift downstream.

down the body of a tube fly with a hot needle. Thread the leader through this and down the tube and tie it to the treble in the normal way. Fished on a tight line, the tube will skate through the surface.

Riffling (and Dibbling) require some finesse. The speed of the lure is important: it should create a wake but should not splash and rip across the surface. Sometimes handlining is used to manoeuvre the fly through the lie. Cast down and across the stream and as the fly nears the lie, strip in line to accelerate its passage and move it in an upstream arc over the fish. In both dibbling and riffling it is essential to vary the speed of the fly and the route it takes over the lie. This is done with a combination of rod tip movement and handlining. Sometimes the fish will take when the fly is skating fast; at other times, when it is dawdling. Sometimes salmon find the riffled fly most attractive when it passes them from below in an upstream direction. It pays to search the lies with different approaches, varying the speed and angles of the fly.

Hooking and Landing the Salmon

It is important not to strike when a salmon takes the fly. Striking fish off is one of the most common blunders committed by the novice, especially if the novice is a trout angler. Unlike the trout, the salmon hooks itself. When a pull is felt, do nothing. Keep the rod still. When the fish swims away, raise the rod steadily without jerking and then play the fish.

Wherever you are fishing, always work out beforehand where you will land your fish. The best places to choose are shelving sand or

The Portland Hitch and (right) the Riffling Tube

gravel beaches. Where there is no beach, select a deep quiet spot where you can use your net. Have the net placed on the bank ready for action.

Use of the gaff is not recommended. Why violate a beautiful fish by sticking a meat hook into it?

There are two golden rules to observe when playing a salmon:
1. Never let the fish see you. Keep out of sight. Insist that your gillie does the same.
2. Never force the fish.

Keep well away from the water and don't try to land the fish too soon. Sometimes a fish will allow itself to be brought close in during the initial stages of play. This apparent submission is not unusual and needs careful management. It is a time of danger. At such moments, instead of lunging with a net, keep out of sight, well back. The fish is only dimly aware of his trouble, but should he see you and become scared, he will resist to the limit of his strength. There are exceptions of course, but in general a frightened fish will fight far longer than one that is merely puzzled, having never seen the angler. Indeed, provided they have not been frightened, many salmon abandon the struggle quite quickly, especially if they have been treated to a 'walking' session up the pool.

It is advisable to 'walk' a fish (whether salmon or sea trout) whenever you are in a position to do so. It takes the heart out of the fish and, by reducing his resistance, shortens the fight.'Walking' can sometimes prevent a fish from running into a snag, or from leaving a pool; it may also prevent a fish from rejoining and scaring other members of a shoal.

The moment a fish is hooked, turn away and begin to walk upstream. The rod is held steady, with the butt set firmly against the body, the point at an angle of about 45° to the water and right angles to the river. No attempt is made to pull the fish along, or to bully him.

If steady progress is maintained upstream the fish will follow quietly. He will, in fact, often gain ground, so that by the time a previously selected landing place is reached, he is somewhere out in the middle of the river and conveniently opposite the rod. You are now in the best place for playing the fish and bringing matters to a conclusion. If he has been 'walked' far, most of the playing has been done.

Where there is a convenient place for beaching a salmon, no landing tackle is needed. When the salmon is beaten the angler draws it ashore not by reeling in, but by walking backwards. When the fish is lying on its side with its head aground the fight is ended and you can relax. Any further movement by the fish will tend to push him further up the beach. If the fish is to be netted, manoeuvre it towards the previously selected area where your net is waiting. Sink the net deep and slide it under the fish. Note that the net is a trap which the fish does not see until he is in it. Never jab the net at a fish or splash with it. This will scare the fish and prolong the fight, giving the hook an opportunity to fall out.

A salmon has taken the fly in the fast water at the neck of the pool. Now the angler must regain the bank and follow downstream to apply sidestrain.

CHAPTER FOUR

SPINNING

On the face of it, spinning seems so much easier than fly fishing. It is true that the novice can learn how to hurl a heavy spinner out across a big river in a matter of minutes, whereas it may take several lessons and a great deal of practice to master the casting of the fly. However, such apparent simplicity in its use belies the fact that to spin effectively demands water knowledge (understanding the river, its underwater contours, the vagaries of the flow, and the likely positions of the fish) as well as tactical acumen (what spinning bait to use in different circumstances, and also the best speed and depth at which to fish).

Most anglers who spin appear to believe that if their lure is flung as far as possible and then reeled back, the rest is up to the salmon.

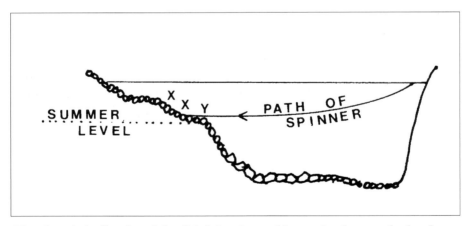

The river is in flood and the fish lying in a taking strip close to the bank. The fly can be fished slowly round. But the spinner is likely to snag bottom as it approaches the taking strip. To avoid this the spin-fisher is tempted to recast just before his lure reaches the fish!

This is not the case. Nor is it true, as so many beginners are convinced, that spinning is invariably more productive than fly fishing. Often, on many rivers, where the fish are lying near to the bank, in the so-called 'taking strip', the fly is the more effective method to use.

It is when the river is high that, with his more sensitive tackle, the experienced fly-fisher comes into his own. As we shall see, only by angling with similar understanding and skill can the spinning man hope to equal his success.

Spinning Tackle
Because many anglers use their spinning tackle also for worm and shrimp/prawn fishing, much of what we recommend below applies also to fishing those two baits.

Spinning Rods
For warm water spinning in summer with small Mepps, light spoons and plugs a rod of about nine feet with a test curve of 1-1½ lb, taking lines of eight to 12 pounds test and capable of casting weights up to about one ounce.

For cold water spring and autumn fishing, and for fishing big rivers in flood, with heavier spinners, plugs and spoons and where extra weight may be required, a rod of 10 feet in length, with a test curve of 2½lb -3lbs, taking lines of 15-25 pounds test and capable of casting weights of three ounces.

Spinning Reels
Fixed spool reels are the most popular for spinning (as well as fishing the worm and shrimp/prawn), but check the following before purchase. A good fixed spool reel should have:

a) a handle on the left hand side (for right handed anglers); if you are left handed check that the handle can be changed over to the other side;

b) adequate spool capacity: many reels are provided with two spools, one for lighter lines and one for heavier lines. For salmon fishing you will need a pair of spools, each holding at least 200 yards of line, one filled with about 10 pound test line and the other with 20 pound test line for the heavier rod.

c) an accessible and easy to use anti-reverse switch (this prevents the handle moving backwards and giving line) that can rapidly be flicked on or off with one finger; some anti-reverse switches are positioned under the handle (in an awkward position) or are very stiff.

d) a drag/slipping clutch system that gives line smoothly and can be adjusted as necessary when a fish is being played.

e) a reel pick-up/bale arm incorporating a roller that prevents the line being frayed when reeling in.

One major problem with the fixed spool reel is that it tends to twist the line. When loaded incorrectly or when a fish is played incorrectly there can be so much line twist that the line becomes a mass of kinks and tangles.

Putting Line on Fixed Spool Reels
Always attach the reel to a rod before filling the spool and feed the line to the reel through the rod rings.

Attach the end of the line to the empty spool with the reel knot. Have someone hold the spool 'face on' and reel on the line fairly tightly, checking that there are no slack turns into which later tight turns could become buried.

Fill the spool to capacity: to overfill may mean that loops fall from the reel and cause tangles; to underfill will result in a reduction of casting range.

If a reel spool has a capacity greater than is required it may be worth putting some heavier line on the spool first as 'backing' and then filling the spool up with the lighter line. Attach the two lines with the Loop-to-Loop Knot.

Note: Several yards of line will be lost from the reel during a day's fishing. Also, should the end of the line show any signs of fraying, cut away the frayed length. Eventually the level of line on the spool will need topping up. Either take off the entire line (run it across a grassy field) and add extra backing or remove some of the old line and add 100 yards of new line to the reel.

Playing Fish with Fixed Spool Reels

Never turn the reel handle to retrieve line when the hook is snagged on the bottom, or a fish is lying on the bottom and not moving, or when a fish is swimming away.

If you do, in a 4:1 geared reel every turn of the handle will result in the slipping clutch adding four turns or twists to the line. This will quickly ruin the line.

There are two ways of playing a fish on the fixed spool reel and also reducing this excessive line twist:

Fixed-spool reel. Note how the line on a correctly filled spool sits directly below the lip.

a) Using the Slipping Clutch
Before starting to fish set the clutch so that it gives line by 'slipping'. Have someone hold the end of the line (or tie it to a post) and pull steadily, at the same time adjusting the drag/clutch knob so that the clutch slips when the rod is flexed to about 90° and you continue to pull. If, when playing the fish the setting is too tight or too slack, alter by turning the clutch knob (see *d above*).

When a big fish is hooked, reel in line ONLY when the fish is running or is heading towards you. If the fish is swimming away, allow it to take line without turning the handle: the clutch will slip as it gives line. If you want to put pressure on the fish, press down on the front of the reel spool with the forefinger of the right hand (right handed anglers) to increase drag; when the fish is tiring, clamp the spool tightly with the finger to draw the fish closer for netting. NEVER turn the handle unless you are gaining line.

b) Using the Reel Handle instead of the Slipping Clutch

Tighten the clutch fully before starting to fish.

When a big fish takes the bait, flick off the anti-reverse so that the handle will turn in both directions. If the fish swims away then let the handle revolve backwards to give line. Pressure can be put on the fish by pressing against the back of the revolving reel drum with one finger; when the fish is tiring, clamp the drum tightly with the finger to draw the fish closer for netting. Turn the handle to gain line ONLY when there is line to be gained.

Removing line twist

A revolving spinner will cause line twist as it spins through the water. We can reduce this to some extent by using a swivel or anti-kink vane (see below). But after a long day of spinning there will be some line twist and a danger of the line kinking.

At the first signs of the line kinking because of excessive twist stop fishing, detach terminal tackle, and remove some of the twists by fixing a split shot or piece of plasticine to the end of the line, opening the bale arm and letting the line drift off downstream a few yards at a time, allowing a few minutes to elapse after every length has been released so that kinks can untwist in the flow. When about 50 yards of line has been released, hold the line in the flow for several minutes and then reel in steadily.

Multiplier Reels

Though more commonly used in saltwater fishing, these reels are considered by many to be the best type for spinning. Multipliers are geared centre pin reels (where one turn of the reel handle produces several turns of the reel spool), with a switch that enables the reel drum to run smoothly for long casts and a variable drag system that is used when a fish is being played. These reels are used 'upside down':

The multiplier reel is fished uppermost on the rod and braked with the thumb.

the rod is held with reel and rod rings uppermost.

Multipliers are easy to use once the angler has mastered the arts of:

a) casting without the spool over-running and causing a 'bird's nest'. As the cast is made the thumb is held over the revolving spool and brakes the spool as the bait approaches landing. When the bait hits the water, the thumb stops the spool.

b) setting the drag correctly. Set up the tackle with the bait to be used hanging on the end of the line with rod held horizontally. Then flip the rod up and down and adjust the drag so that the bait just fails to pull off line and descend to the ground.

Practice with both reels is essential, both for distance casts, but especially for accuracy. In heavily wooded becks, where the fish often lie below overhanging bushes, most anglers fail to catch, not because they cannot cast far enough, but because they cannot cast accurately.

Spinners, spoons and plugs

Sometimes these three categories of lures are all referred to as 'spinners'. But they differ in their structure and action in the water.

+ Spinners have a body or spoon that revolves or spins around a central axis (Devon minnow, Mepps).

+ Spoons do not (or should not) revolve or spin; their action should be a flickering, undulating motion as they pass through the water (Toby). If they spin they are being fished too quickly.

+ Plugs also do not spin: They usually have an erratic movement through the water. Some plugs are floaters that dive when line is

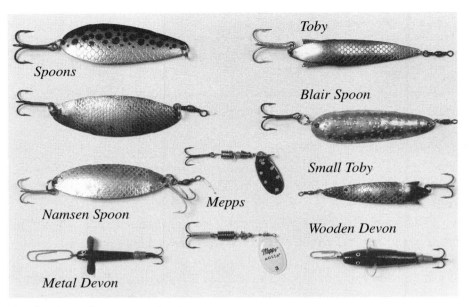

A selection of spoons and spinners

retrieved and surface when it is not (these are the best for salmon fishing in most rivers where the salmon are lying in less than six feet of water); others are sinkers.

Spinners, plugs and spoons are expensive, yet some manufacturers use very inferior materials. Below is a selection of recommended lures:

Recommended Spinning Baits

1. The Devon Minnow

These come in metal, plastic and wood, in sized from one to nearly four inches, and in almost every colour and combination of colours. In slacker water the wooden and plastic versions tend to swim better, since metal Devons are liable to sag taildown at low speeds.

2. The Toby Spoon

This is the best fish attractor we have ever used - and the worst hooker! Like all long spoons (including the Rapala Inkoo), it can be improved by fixing the treble to a short trace.

3. The Mepps Spoon

This is an excellent lure. The low-friction bearing permits the blade to flutter most attractively when fished at very low speeds - a great advantage.

The Mepps is the best lure we know for upstream fishing when a spate river is dropping and clearing after a rise of water, and particularly good in its small sizes for hooking grilse.

4. The Flying-C

This is a superb lure. It has an attractive fluttering blade. It has weight, can be cast much further than the Mepps and fishes deep. The long rubber tails add extra movement.

The Flying-C is especially effective in deep, slow pools where it is essential to get the lure down quickly.

5. The Kynoch Killer

If you go harling, this (together with the Rapala) is probably your best bait. It has a most eccentric and unlikely action. When you first launch the thing and watch it zooming about as it disappears into the depths astern of the boat, you tend to shrug your shoulders. But don't be misled. It is very effective.

6. The Rapala

Rapalas come in a wide range of sizes, weights and sinking rates. For salmon angling in shallow, boulder strewn rivers the basic floating Rapalas are the best, both in the jointed and one piece versions. In deeper pools the sinking Countdown Rapalas are ideal. In low, clear water the 2" and 2½" are ideal on the lighter rod. In heavier, coloured water the 4⅜" and 5½" models. Colours? Of the wide range available, the blue and silver, and brown and silver are very effective in clear water, the brown and gold, and gold and fluorescent red in coloured water.

Knots: Use tucked blood knots.

Fishing spoons, spinners and plugs

Many anglers simply tie a spinner to the end of their line and cast it out onto the water. Then they reel it back, hoping that some fish will

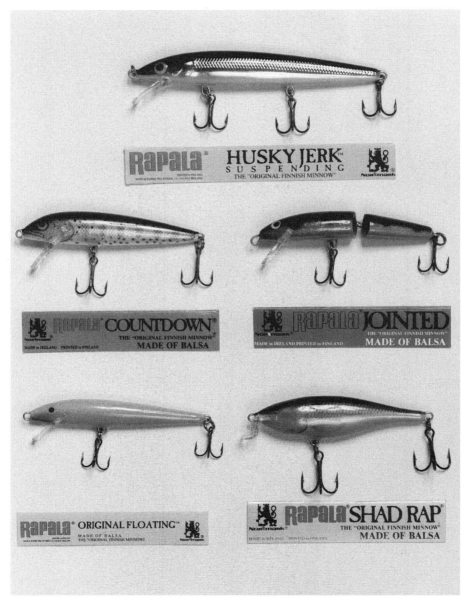

A selection of Rapala lures. These are available in a wide range of sizes and colours.

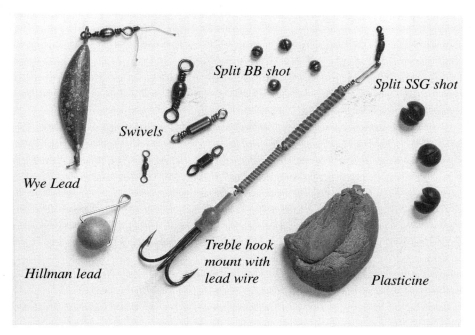

Weights and swivels from MG's tackle bag

take hold. It is worth, however, giving more thought to the rig so that the spinner is fished more effectively.

To reduce the problem of line twist while spinning you will need a swivel between line and leader. There are two main types:

Barrel Swivels

The most popular and readily available, but very inefficient. The 'three-way' version is essential for paternoster spinning rigs.

Ball-bearing Swivels

Though expensive, they are the best.

Anti-kink Vanes

These are essential when fishing very fast water with revolving spinning baits (such as the Devon minnows). They comprise a celluloid or plastic, half-moon or rectangular vane attached to a swivel. Most are produced with barrel swivels attached, the best (and most expensive) have ball-bearing swivels attached.

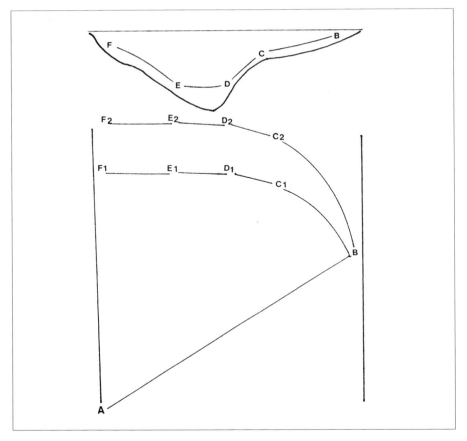

Manipulating a heavy spinning bait through a pool with variations of depth and flow rate

Always attach the reel line to the wire loop of the anti-kink vane, and the leader to the swivel.

2. Often it is essential to add weight to a spinning rig. This weight may:

a) allow the spinner to be fished more deeply, or,

b) help the spinner to be fished more slowly in fast, turbulent water - the extra weight will prevent the light spinner being dragged or skated by the flow.

There are two ways of adding weight to a spinning rig: adding weight to the spinner itself (or using a heavier spinner), or fixing weight to the line.

5. Adding weight to the spinner or using a heavier spinner

One great advantage that this approach has over fixing weight to the line is accuracy in casting. One can cast much more accurately over all distances when the weight is concentrated in one place, i.e. in the bait.

The disadvantage is that, when fishing deep, too heavy a bait will snag whilst too light a bait will not fish deeply enough. One needs experience of the water and of the weight to be used. When weight is being fixed on the line above the spinner, then it can be more easily modified to take into account slight changes in depth and flow, especially when a plasticine paternoster rig is being used.

Another great advantage is that it is much easier to manipulate a spinner when there is no extra weight on the line.

The angler at A casts at 45° (see previous page) down and across a pool to B. Initially the spinner is working through fairly shallow but very fast water. So, keeping the rod tip high and back-reeling, the spinner fishes slowly across the band of fast water but at the same time drops downstream in arc B-C1. At C1 the water deepens and slows. Now the angler quickly lowers the rod tip and stops back-winding. The spinner dives deeply between C1 and D1, and flutters across the bottom of the deep water but then, at E1, the angler lifts the rod tip and the spinner rises between E1 and F1. Now the angler begins slowly to reel in before making the next cast.

Salmon are likely to take in the drop-back B-C1, in the C1-D1 dive and in the rise E1-F1.

On the next cast the spinner may be cast again to B, but this time the reel is back-wound slightly faster so that it swings down and across the stream in arc B-C2; the rod tip is held high. Then, with the spinner at C2 the rod tip is lowered and spinner dives through C2-D2. At E2 the rod tip is lifted and the spinner rises between E2 and F2 before being slowly retrieved. B-C2, C2-D2 and E2-F2 are main taking zones.

This is a most effective way of fishing many salmon pools. But the angler must know the positions of lies, depth and flow variations and the ideal weight of spinner to use.

Adding weight: In Devon minnows, fine lead wire can be wound around the hook trace.

If fishing Rapalas, the lighter floating ones can be used in very shallow water, the Countdown in deeper water, and in very deep water the Shad Rap.

If fishing Tobies, a heavier one can be used, e.g. 18g instead of a 12g.

Fixing weight to the line above the spinner:

Some anglers simply fix heavy shot (e.g. SSG) to the line, or thread the line through a hollow lead. It is more effective to use leads specially designed for spinning. The best types of weight to use are:

Hillman Weights

These are drilled bullets that clip onto the upper eye of the swivel (the eye to which the reel-line is attached).

Wye Weights

Designed originally for spinning for salmon in big rivers, these leads incorporate a swivel. They are tied between reel-line and leader. Fix them with the weight close to the reel-line and the Wye weight swivel close to the leader.

These spinning weights not only add the necessary weight but they also help reduce line twist provided that the weight is always above the swivel, attached to the reel-line. Other weights do not have this advantage.

A deep, streamy, boulder-strewn pool-neck holds several salmon, but the weight needed to take the spinner down to the fish tends to snag, with the consequent loss of weight and bait. The following rig is the answer:

The reel-line and leader are tied to the opposite eyes of a three-way swivel. A length (up to three feet) of very weak nylon is attached to

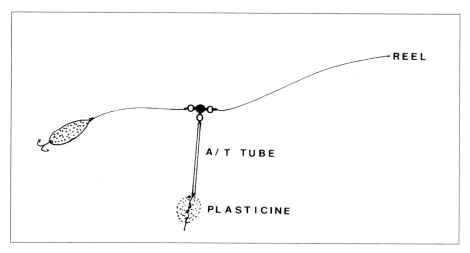

The Snaggy, Fast-Water Plasticine Paternoster Rig.

the other eye of the swivel and threaded through a length of narrow anti-tangle ledger-tube. Where the end of this line protrudes, tie a few plain overhand knots and then mould a lump of plasticine over these knots and the into end of the ledger tube. Use a buoyant bait (e.g. wooden Devon, floating Rapala). Cast out into the deep snaggy water. The plasticine weight will hold bottom, leaving the bait fishing off the bottom, in front of the fish's nose. Should the plasticine snag, a pull will release the line with just the loss of harmless plasticine.

CHAPTER 5

MORE ABOUT THE SPINNER

Spinning involves far more than casting and retrieving a bait. Or, at least, effective spinning does. In fact, effective spinning is as difficult as fly-fishing. Perhaps more so. By using a lightweight fly and varying the density of the flyline, the fly fisherman can fish the fly at the depth that is likely to be most effective. And by using a variety of 'tricks'- such as mending, working the fly, varying the angle of cast, and backing-up - the fly fisherman can vary the speed of the fly. He can fish the fly very slowly in very shallow water.

By contrast, most spinners are heavy and tend to sink if fished slowly. And spinners are very expensive compared to flies. The last thing the spin-fisherman wants is to lose his precious lures. So, when the spinner comes round to shallowing water under the bank, he reels it in as quickly as possible to prevent it snagging. He avoids runs that are shallow and boulder-strewn. And in so doing he loses few lures and catches few fish.

Presentation of the spinner.
Just as fly-fishing can be divided into the two general systems of cold water: big fly fished deep, and warm water: small fly fished close to the surface, so too can spinning.

In early spring (January to April) and late autumn (October and November) when the water temperature is less than about 48°F, a big spinner, fished deep, is most effective.

The choice of spinner might include a 3-3½" Devon minnow, Toby (28 gram), Blair spoon, Countdown Rapala. And extra weight will almost certainly have to be added to take the lure deep.

A shallow rocky run in summer, tricky water for the spin fisherman. Both the line and the spinner sink. The angler must reel in the spinner after every cast and often his lure will snag on rocks.

From late spring to early autumn (late April to October) when water temperatures are higher than about 48°F, a small or medium sized spinner, fished higher in the water, is more effective. The choice of spinner might include 1½"-2½" Devon minnow, Toby (12 gram), Blair spoon, floating Rapala, Mepps (sizes 1-4). Only with the river in flood will there be need to add weight to the spinning rig.

A. *(See diagram, page 72)* In deep, fairly fast water cast the lure down and across the pool (from wading angler at A to B), and keep in touch with the lure as it swings around, over the lies, by very slowly turning the reel handle. The wading angler can lead the lure around below him with the rod (from C to D). Then, as the spinner comes round into slacker water at D its speed is steadily increased. At E the cast is fished out and the lure is reeled in quickly before the next cast is made.

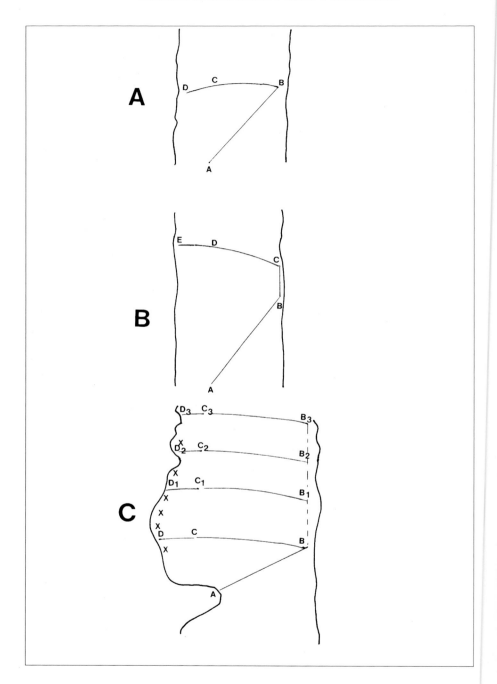

B. In very deep, fast water a larger weight may be needed to take the lure down. But also a modified technique.

Cast the lure down and across the pool (from wading angler at A to B). Release extra line (up to five yards, depending on speed of flow) so that the lure drops down to C with this extra slack. As the current works the lure across from C to D the reel handle is not turned at all. The power of the current will keep everything tight between lure and rod. The angler slowly leads the lure round to E, and then retrieves prior to the next cast.

C. The river Eden has some 'pots', six feet and more in depth and with a fast turbulent flow going through them, that hold spring salmon. The fish lie off the main current, often very close to the bank. Here a floating bait is ideal (e.g. 3" wooden Devon, or floating Rapala) with all the weight on the line (a big Wye lead or, better, the 'snaggy, fast-water, plasticine paternoster rig').

The angler stands on a rocky outcrop at the head of the pot (A), and casts out the lure to B. The lure swims quickly across the main flow

Deep fast water spinning a pool neck

until, at C, the weight is felt bouncing across the bottom. If the weight does not bounce on the bottom at C, then more must be added until it does: here, plasticine has the advantage for it is easy to add extra. Now the floating lure, fishing off the bottom, swings inshore and is led round by the angler tight under the bank (D) before being retrieved.

The next cast is made to B, but this time an extra three yards of line is released so that the lure falls downstream to B1. Again the lure washes quickly across the main current, until the weight bounces on the bottom at C1. The lure is then fished through the lies to D1.

And so, from this one position the pot is fished out with an extra six yards of line being released on cast C2, D2, nine yards on cast C3,D3 and so on.

Several lures will be lost during the day (especially if Wye leads are used). But that expense is essential if the pot is to be fished effectively.

A. *Spinning in varied currents*

In deep fast water the lure is best cast down and across the flow from A. The reel handle is turned very, very slowly simply to keep in touch with the lure, that swings across the flow.

In slower water the lure is best cast directly across or very slightly downstream of the angler at B. Here the current is too slow to work the lure, so the angler reels it slowly back.

B. *Round-the-clock fishing with a Flying-C*

This is an ideal way of fishing a big, deep slow pool. Starting at A1, the angler casts, in turn, to B1, then C1, then D1 and so on. After each cast the angler retrieves the heavy Flying-C rapidly. He then moves to A2, and repeats fishing round-the – clock with casts to B2, C2, D2 and so on. A salmon lying at X may refuse the spinner when retrieved after cast D1, but when covered by cast B2 it may take.

C. *Upstream clear-water spinning with a small Mepps*

In low, crystal clear water it is very easy to scare the fish...and a scared salmon will rarely be caught. So the angler starts at the bottom of the pool at A, keeping low (on hands and knees if necessary). A gold or copper size 0, 1 or 2 Mepps is the ideal lure.

The spinner is cast up and across the stream and retrieved quickly until, at B1, it starts to swing round towards the rod tip. Now the speed of retrieve is slowed down as the lure swims back to the rod on the arc B1, C. Salmon (and sea trout) usually take fiercely in the first part of the arc, B1,B2.

d. Two-way fishing with a Rapala

This is the ideal way of fishing narrow pool necks on a falling spate, when fish are running and resting for a few moments on their upstream journey. Or fishing long, narrow, tree-girt pools on small spate rivers. It is also a great way of catching sea trout at dawn, after a night's fly-fishing.

In deep, turbulent water a 2½" or 3½" Countdown Rapala is ideal. In steadier flows the 3⅛" Husky Jerk. In shallower, boulder-strewn water, a 2½" or 3½" floating Rapala. Silver, gold and blue (the latter is especially good for sea trout) are three useful choices for clear water, but in coloured water gold/fluorescent red, perch and (Husky

Upstream spinning in slow clear water.

75

Two way fishing the Rapala. The angler has cast down and across. He leads the lure across the flow,taking the rod in his left hand and extending the left arm to complete the 'lead'. Extra line is released and the angler then leads the lure back to his right

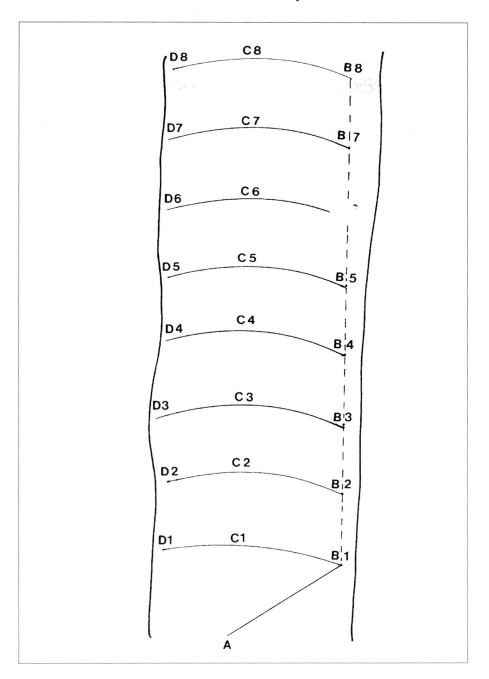

Jerk) orange crawdad appear to be more effective.

(See diagram, p77) The angler takes up position A at the head of the pool neck. The lure is cast down and across the flow to B1, and allowed to flicker across the flow WITHOUT ANY RETRIEVE. Note that the flickering, wobbling action of the Rapala, that fish find so attractive, is produced in the slowest of flows. When the lure comes round to C1, immediately downstream of the angler, it is led across by the rod and extended arm to D1. The lure is then led back by the angler using extended arm and rod through C1 to B1.

A yard of line is then stripped from the reel and the lure drifts downstream to B2. It is then led round through C2 to D2, and then back to B2. Another yard of line is released and the lure fished two-way on the arc B3, C3, D3 and so on.

When the pool neck has been fished out (the lure is now at D8), instead of retrieving the lure, the angler reels in a yard of line at a time and two-way fishes the lure up the pool neck.

A salmon (or sea trout) that has refused the lure flickering across from one direction will sometimes take it boldly as it returns from the other direction. And a fish that refused the lure as it was worked down a pool will sometimes take as the lure is fished back up the pool.

CHAPTER 6

WORM FISHING

A high proportion of 'fly-only' game-fishers argue that other methods are too easy and too effective. Especially worm and shrimp/prawn fishing. Not so! As W.C. Stewart rightly pointed out in *The Practical Angler* (1857):

'Those anglers who despise worm-fishing as a thing so simple as to be quite unworthy of their attention, would quickly discover their mistake if brought to a small clear water on a warm sunny day in June or July.'

Worm fishing tackle

The object is to present the worm in such a way that it behaves as naturally as possible, drifting downstream with the current without drag or hindrance. A light single-handed rod of at least 10 feet in length is ideal, though there are some purpose-built spinning and shrimping rods of 11-12 feet on the market that are excellent. These slightly longer rods help in holding the line high above strong flows that might otherwise pull the bait out of position; they help in leading the line round obstacles (such as boulders).

The reel should hold up to 200 yards of 15-20 lb test monofilament nylon or braided Dacron.

Most anglers today use fixed-spool reels exclusively. But for low water worming on smaller rivers a centre-pin reel has the edge. As we have witnessed on numerous occasions, a salmon frequently nudges a worm a number of times before taking it inside its mouth. It is when a fish is toying with a bait in this fashion that the advantage of the centre-pin reel becomes apparent. Time and again the worm must cover exactly the same spot. This is difficult to accomplish with anything but a reel which has the exact length of line already stripped off.

On the end of the mainline is tied a small swivel, and on its other eye a three foot leader of lighter nylon, 10-15 lb test. On the end of the leader is either a three-hook Stewart tackle, two-hook Pennell tackle or a single hook.

The Worm

As an all-round salmon bait, nothing beats the blue-headed lobworm *Allolobophora longa*, a common resident of riverside pastures, vegetable plots and lawns.

For high water worming, one lobworm on a size 10 hook or up to six lobworms on a size 2-4 hook are ideal.

For low water worming, one lobworm on a Stewart or Pennell tackle is ideal for both salmon and sea trout fishing in fast, streamy water. In gin-clear, slower, summer pools, where sea trout are likely to dominate the catch, a single brandling or redworm on a size 12-14 hook is an effective combination (but use a 6 lb leader).

Weight

The art of worm fishing is to trundle the bait downstream along the river bed. In very shallow, slow flows no weight may be required. But in faster water weight must be added: just enough to take the bait down, yet not so much that it snags on the bottom. Correctly mounted, the weight or bait will be felt bumping on the bottom occasionally as it moves downstream.

Although split-shot are popularly used, the ideal weight is plasticine. Mould some round the line, just above the swivel. According to the water flow, tiny plasticine beads can be added or removed to give the perfect weight for each lie.

The other advantage of plasticine over split-shot is that, should it snag between boulders, a pull will often release the line and only the plasticine be lost. If split-shot become snagged, then weight, leader and hook are lost.

Pennell and Stewart Tackles can be tied at home, but are equally easy to tie at the end of the leader at the waterside. The Pennell tackle has two hooks, the Stewart three.

High Water Worming

With a river in flood the fish will lie out of the main flow, and often very close to the bank in slack or almost slack water. Good high water lies include the inside of bends (over shingle that is normally high-and-dry), sandy bays, tight under the bank (if the river is very high, even amongst what is usually bankside vegetation).

The major difficulty is finding these high-water lies. When the river is in flood, fish rarely show themselves. The ideal approach,

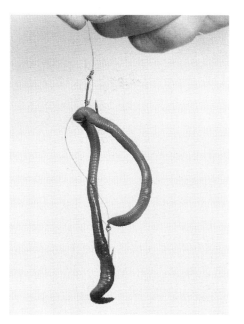

Pennell tackle baited with a blue-headed lob worm

therefore, is to travel light and fish as many potential lies as possible, making sure that each lie is approached with great care. The fish are close in and, although you cannot see them, they will be able to detect heavy footfalls and see an angler moving through even the most turbid water. So keep well back, cast the worm out into the edge of the main flow. As the bait swings into the lie, the amount of weight should be sufficient to take it bumping across the bottom.

You should be able to feel the bait fishing correctly. After casting hold a loop of line between thumb and forefinger of the non-rod hand. The pads of thumb and finger are very sensitive: you will feel when the bait or weight touches the bottom, or when a leaf nudges the line, or a salmon takes. If the bait swings around freely then add more weight. If the bait hits the bottom and stops without bouncing round into the lie, take off some weight.

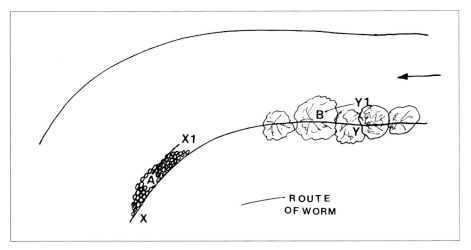

Presenting a worm (1). Here are two high water lies, one over shingle which is high and dry in low water (lie A) and one under some alders where water depth is less than a foot in low water (lie B). There is three feet on the gauge. The fish are lying in two feet in slack water (lie A) and a maximum of four feet of slow-flowing water (lie B). Lie A is fished from point X. But because the fish are in very shallow water, close to the bank, the angler must approach carefully and fish in a kneeling position. The bait is cast out to X1 and slowly trundles across into the lie.

Lie B is fished from point Y. Here the angler takes full advantage of cover. The bait is flicked out and when it has come around under the bank, extra line is fed out, a little at a time, so that the bait moves downstream in the slow flow and through the lie. Note that, when fishing this lie, the angler may not be able to see much (he is hiding behind the tree at Y); but he will be able to feel what is happening through the thumb and forefinger of his non-rod hand. When a fish is hooked, he nips round the tree to play it.

Low Water Worming

In high summer, when the river is low, salmon and sea trout often lie in shallow, boulder-strewn runs. Many of the fish will be lying in water only two or three feet deep. Much of it will be wadeable. But wade only when it is necessary. Don't start by fishing the distant water. Always fish the lies close to your own bank before wading and casting further out. Don't be in too much of a hurry. Fish slowly and carefully. You cannot over-fish a salmon lie - provided you fish with care. Although you have covered a salmon a number of times unsuccessfully, it may take later, if you haven't walked on top of it.

Note: If the angler stands too far upstream of the lie it is difficult to prevent drag. Too far downstream, and the worm will not precede the line.

The order in which to fish three possible salmon lies by a rock. Before starting to fish water of this sort, time should always be spent in careful examination, snags and probable lies being noted.

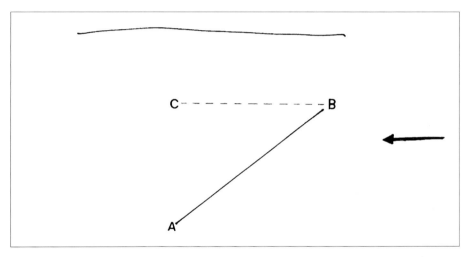

Presenting a worm (2). The angler at A stands just upstream of the lie at C and casts to B. The worm sinks as it washes down with the current between B and C. AC is shorter than AB, so that the angler must shorten line as the worm comes dowstream, by drawing in line with the noncasting hand.

Very seldom is such water fished down straight from top to bottom, or straight up from bottom to top. The angler should move about carefully, now up, now down, according to the particular lie he wishes to cover. The order in which the lies are fished is of great importance.

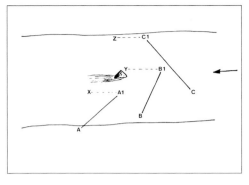

Presenting a worm (3) 1.Cast to point A1 to catch Fish X. This operation will not disturb the other lies. 2. Move upstream and fish the lie upstream of the rock (Fish Y) by casting to point B1. Fish Z is difficult to catch, except from the opposite bank. Move still further upstream and cast down-stream to point C1, letting go some slack line. If the fish refuses the worm, guide the line over the rock by holding the rod at arm's length above your head.

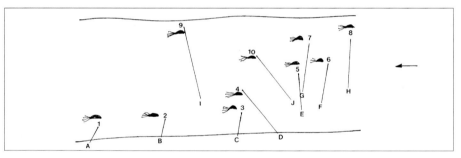

Presenting a worm (4). Ten salmon are lying in a stretch of fast, shallow, clear, broken water. Only by using his water-sense, by 'reading' the water, could an angler decide where the fish were lying. Lies 1, 2 and 3 should be fished first (from points A, B and C respectively). Then lies 4, 5 and 6 (from D, E and F). After this the further lies can be fished, 7 and 8 from G and H. The fish lying at 9 is virtually uncatchable (except from the opposite bank) unless the angler wades in above lie 2 (to point I). But if he does this he will certainly frighten away the fish lying at 1 and 2 which, if they have already refused the worm but remain undisturbed, may take later in the day. Unless the fish takes on the first cast, he is almost certain to get snagged. This fish is best left until later. There is a good chance of covering 10 satisfactorily. It is now safe for the angler to wade to point J, since he is well below the fish in lie 3. He can turn a long and difficult cast into a relatively easy one.

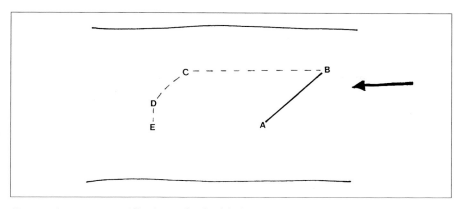

Presenting a worm (5). A method of fishing a moving worm in deeper water is to cast well upstream with just enough weight on the leader to take the bait to the bottom. The worm should sink to depth and then swing very slowly round in front of the fish. This is a most effective method when the river has fallen back to summer level after a spate that has brought shoals of fresh fish into the pools.

Of a number of salmon at any particular moment, only one or two (if any) may be taking fish. Obviously the more fish the angler covers, the more chance he has of covering a taker. Although every salmon refuses his worm the first time he fishes the water, he may very well hook one later - provided he has not frightened it out of its lie.

Hooking fish on worm

Salmon can take the worm in a variety of ways. They may grab it, hook themselves and immediately go tearing off across the river. But more often the take is quieter and more subtle. Through thumb and forefinger of the non-rod hand, holding the line, the angler may feel a grating sensation - it might be a fish, but is it a leaf caught on the line? There may be a short pull, and then nothing. The line may simply stop - has it snagged bottom? Wait. Do nothing. The salmon may be holding the worm in the front of its jaw. Strike and the worm will be pulled away. Within a few seconds (usually 20-30) a more positive pull will be felt as the salmon moves off. Now is the time to tighten into the fish.

Sea trout generally take the worm more positively than salmon. There will be one or two hard 'knocks'. Again, do nothing. But then, within five or 10 seconds there will be a firm pull as the fish moves away with the worm. Tighten and the fish will be hooked.

Regardless of what comes naturally, the most successful anglers are those who have developed their water-sense: that ability to examine a stretch of fishing and decide unerringly where fish are likely to be lying.

By those fortunate enough to have the opportunity, water-sense begins to be absorbed during childhood. To the late starter it is not so easily acquired, and books alone are of little help. There is no substitute for experience at the waterside, preferably in the company of a top-class fisherman.

Sensitive finger pads keep the angler in touch with the worm

It is like learning a new language. Gradually, what has seemed meaningless becomes significant, and certain spots will stand out as being more attractive than others. Aided by water-sense, the novice will find himself taking salmon and sea trout with the worm from water which, previously, he would have walked past without a second glance.

CHAPTER 7

PRAWN AND SHRIMP FISHING

Whilst both prawns and shrimps are effective baits throughout the salmon fishing season, in general big 'prawns' are perhaps the ideal bait to use in colder water conditions and in bigger, faster rivers: for instance, prawn was the bait to use in the mighty rivers of Norway before the present ban. By contrast, the smaller 'shrimps' are perhaps the best bait to use in summer and early autumn, when the water is warm, and in smaller rivers. Indeed, in most rivers of the British Isles the shrimp is used almost exclusively today, and not the big prawn. For this reason we will refer to both baits as 'shrimps': if you wish to try a prawn, then what is said below applies equally.

Fishing the Shrimp

In general the shrimp is not an 'in' lure. The use of this humble bait has been almost universally condemned by the pundits as harmful, 'unsporting', and quite beyond the pale.

It has been argued that salmon will often flee a pool when a prawn is cast to them. It has further been argued that the shrimp is so easy to fish and so deadly that it should be banned on the grounds of conservation. Neither argument is correct. Shrimp fishing is a skilful and fascinating technique, especially in low clear water when both shrimp and salmon can be seen. That the shrimp catches salmon there is no doubt. But there is nothing magical about its powers; many salmon are unimpressed by its allure.

As to salmon fleeing a pool: the reactions of a salmon to the shrimp (as we have observed them in clear water streams) may be summarised as follows:

1. It remains in its lie and ignores the shrimp. This is, alas, the commonest response.

2. It shows signs of agitation as the shrimp approaches: the fins quiver, the mouth and gills flare, the body shudders. But the fish remains in its lie. This is the second commonest response.

3. It shows signs of agitation as the shrimp approaches, eventually abandoning its lie, and often leaping further up or down the pool. (It is probably this behaviour that has given rise to the hair-raising stories of salmon fleeing from a pool.) The salmon does not usually stay away from its lie for very long - usually from two to 10 minutes.

4. It swims up as though to intercept the shrimp, but turns away without touching it and returns to its lie.

Note: We have observed these same responses (1-4) to the fly and to the worm.

5. It sucks the shrimp into its mouth and immediately blows it out again, leaving no mark on it.

6. It nips the shrimp, contriving to shave off the whiskers and sometimes part of the head or a tiny part of the back, or the eggs from the belly.

7. It takes the shrimp in its mouth, crushes it, and then blows it out again.

Note: In responses 5, 6 and 7, the fish is not hooked, and usually the angler is unaware of what has happened unless he can see both bait and salmon. Even response (7), which appears to be quite violent, is rarely felt through the line or registered by the float.

8. It takes the shrimp fiercely, either by grabbing it as it swings past or by sucking it up off the bottom.

9. It chases the length of the pool to grab the shrimp.

Note: In responses 8 and 9, the fish is hooked, usually in the jaw, occasionally inside the mouth. But in both cases it will soon eject the shrimp, so strike smartly.

Tackle for fishing the shrimp
Rods, reels and lines. The shrimp can be fished in exactly the same

Prawn and Shrimp Fishing

way as the fly on the 15 foot fly rod. In this case it is essential to use the wired mounted shrimp.

Anglers fishing the shrimp on fly tackle often find that, after a couple of casts, the bait breaks up. This is because too much force is put into the forward cast. When fishing the shrimp on a fly-rod, use less force on the forward cast so that the shrimp is 'lobbed' rather than punched out over the water.

Many anglers fish the shrimp on spinning tackle. Again, as with fishing shrimp on fly-fishing tackle, this has the advantage that one rod will fish two completely different methods. However there is a great advantage in using a longer rod and a purpose-built shrimp/worm rod, 11-12' in length, together with a centre-pin or fixed spool reel carrying up to 200 yards of 15-20 lb test nylon is a better combination.

A swivel is fixed at the end of the reel-line and a leader of about four feet in length, of lighter nylon (10-15 lb), fixed to the other eye of the swivel.

Floats. The 'pike-bung' has long been popular, but when a fish takes the bait the broad body of this float offers great resistance. The fish must pull hard to drag it under, feels the resistance, and tends to let go of the

bait quickly. Far better are 'cigar-sliders' that have a more slender body, or 'chub-floats'. Select floats that will carry between four and six swan-shot. These will carry the mounted shrimp and the necessary shot to sink the bait.

Weights. For float-fishing, swan-shots are ideal, though, for stret-pegging in snaggy water plasticine is better because it snags less and, when it does, a pull slips the line through the snagged plasticine. For

Slider and bung floats   the same reason, plasticine is the ideal weight to use when free-lining.

Partridge Shrimp/Prawn Pins. These come in four lengths (1", 1½", 2" and 2½") to accommodate different sizes of baits.

Treble Hooks. For smaller shrimps, size 12; for bigger prawns, size 10.

Fine copper wire or fuse wire. For wiring mounts used with the fly-fishing tackle, and for free-lining and stret-pegging.

Fine lead wire. For producing weighted mounts.

20 lb test Alasticum wire. For making mounts.

Small swivels. For making mounts.

Line-Greaser. Essential for float-fishing. This little gadget fits either in the butt-ring of the rod or clamps to the rod just below the butt-ring. It keeps the line above the float greased, so that it floats and can be easily mended.

Shrimps and Mounts. Naturally shrimps (and prawns) are a sandy-grey or sandy-brown colour. Those used for fishing are boiled, and when boiled they turn orange-pink. However, experiments indicate that shrimps are more effective when dyed Windsor purple or ruby-red.

Shrimps are usually purchased pre-dyed, stored in salt in sealed plastic bags. These will last almost indefinitely in a refrigerator.

Shrimp Mounts. There are basically two methods of mounting a shrimp:

1. Long-trotting, float-fishing mount.

A shrimp pin is slid onto the leader and treble hook tied to the end of the leader using Tucked Blood-Knot. The shrimp is straightened and threaded onto the pin via the underside of its tail (or telson).

The shrimp and pin are then slid down the leader to the treble hook, which is fixed by one point under the thorax of the shrimp (in between the legs).

2. Fly-fishing, Stret-pegging, and Free-lining wired mount.

First make the mount.

a. Take a treble hook and one foot length of Alasticum wire. Fix the hook in place and twist wire as shown.

b. A second treble can be attached approximately one third of the

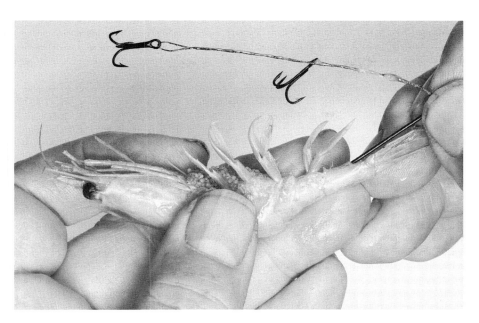

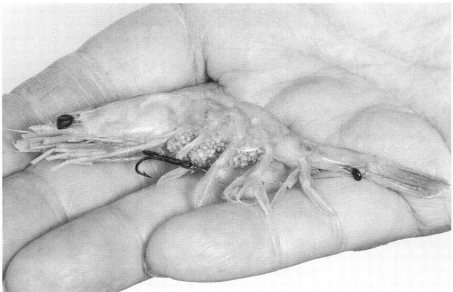

Mounting the shrimp

way along the mount. Such a tandem-hook mount is used only when bigger shrimps/prawns are the intended bait.

c. When the desired length of mount has been achieved, fix a small swivel to the end of the mount. Coat the turnings of wire with epoxy-resin (e.g. Araldite).

d. Take a shrimp-pin, slightly open the eye, fix this on the eye of the swivel - the same eye as the mount - and close the eye to fix the pin in place.

Make several mounts in sizes 1", 1½", 2" and 2½" to accommodate the range of bait sizes.

e. Weight some mounts by twisting fine lead wire around the mounts.

f. To fix shrimp on mount:

(i) thread a one foot length of fine copper or fuse wire through swivel eye;

(ii) insert pin through straightened body of the bait via the under-side of its tail

(iii) fix treble hook(s) in underside of the shrimp;

(iv) secure shrimp onto mount with bindings of fine wire.

The reel-line, whether for fly-fishing, stret-pegging or freelining, is tied to the upper eye of the swivel.

Float-Fishing the Shrimp
The two most effective methods are long-trotting and stret-pegging.
Long-trotting
This is the easiest method of fishing the shrimp - and very effective when fished properly.

This is the ideal method to use in those deep, fairly slow pools that hold good numbers of salmon but do not lend themselves to conventional fly-fishing techniques.
The Long-trotting Rig
A cigar-slider float is slid onto the reel-line, at the end of which a swivel is then tied. A four foot leader is tied to the other eye of the swivel and a Long-trotting mount tied to the end of the leader and a

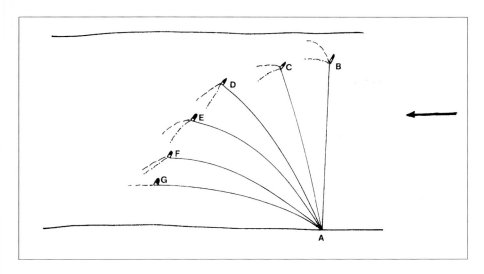

Stret-pegging. The shrimp is cast at right angles from A to B, as soon as the bait has settled it is held back on a tight line for a few seconds. The shrimp trundles across the bottom on a short arc. The line is then released and the float driftd down stream to see where it is again held back. The process continues to G where the bait will come to rest at the edge of fast and slack water.

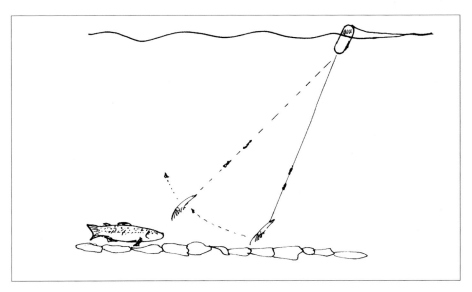

shrimp fixed in place.

STOP-KNOT

CIGAR SLIDER FLOAT

SWIVEL

WEIGHT

MOUNT

The float cannot slide down to the bait because of the swivel; but it can slide, unhindered, up the reel-line. To prevent this, yet allow easy adjustment of depth at which the bait will be fished, a Stop-Knot is tied from a length of heavy nylon above the float. Fix a single swan-shot on the line one foot below the swivel and drop the baited float-rig into deep slack water. If too much float sticks up above the water surface when the rig has settled, fix swan-shot(s) next to the first one.

Long-trotting Presentation

Salmon that are lying on the bottom respond better to a bait fished at or deeper than mid-water to one fished closer to the surface. But bites are more positive, and easier to hook, the further the fish have to rise to take the bait.

Therefore, start with the bait at midwater and gradually increase depth by slipping the stop-knot further up the reel line after a few trots through the lie.

In one deep pool that we know well, water depth in the best lie (that can hold up to 30 salmon) is 14 feet and sometimes the bait must be 12 feet down to entice the fish. Here we begin with a distance of six feet between bait and stop-knot and slowly increase depth by 18 inch increments.

Note: the advantage of using the stop-knot: Where the water is so deep, the stop-knot will slide through the rod-rings and onto the reel, but is cast out without hindrance.

Cast out, let bait, weight and float settle, and slowly trot the bait through the lie. Should a belly of slack line form due to vagaries in the current and start to pull the float off the intended line, mend the line. This is possible only when the line between float and rod tip has been greased.

Salmon will often take a shrimp that slowly drifts downstream. However a most effective method of inducing the salmon to take is to hold-back.

As the shrimp reaches the lie, stop extra line being released from the reel. As the float is held-back, so the shrimp will swing upwards in the flow right in front of the fish. It appears that the inert shrimp, that suddenly 'comes to life', goads the salmon into taking it. When a salmon takes a trotted shrimp, the float usually bobs once or twice and then dips beneath the surface. Tighten as soon as it dips.

Stret-Pegging

This is a float-fishing method for streamy water where the bottom is of sand or very fine gravel. *(see Diagram, p 93)*

Set the distance between float and swan-shots deeper than water depth by about two feet (by sliding the stop-knot up or down the line), and have the distance between swan-shots and shrimp mount about three feet.

1. Cast at right angles across the river (A to B). As soon as the float has landed and shots and bait settled, hold it back on a tight line for a few seconds. The shots and shrimp will trundle across the bottom on a short arc.

2. Release line and allow the float to drift a couple of yards down-stream to C, and then hold back the float for a few seconds more. Continue to release line and hold-back the float at D, then E, F and finally G, where the bait will come to rest at the crease between fast and slack water. Fished in this way the bait covers a wide area.

3. Retrieve through slack water.

Free-lining a Shrimp

A most exciting way of fishing the shrimp in low clear water is to free-line it, with the minimum of weight, to a particular fish. Then both shrimp and salmon are kept in view.

Start off with a weighted mount and later add weight to the line in the form of a small sliver of plasticine or one swan-shot.

Sometimes, if the shrimp can be swung round well below the

salmon, then manoeuvred upstream and left to lie close to a salmon, the fish, after a few minutes of increasing agitation, will suddenly turn and make a ferocious grab at it. A most exciting moment for the angler and anyone else who happens to be watching. Needless to say, both angler and watchers should keep out of sight.

Anyone who considers shrimp fishing to be 'unsporting' may care to reflect that this low-water technique demands a very high degree of angling skill.

No sportsman should unwittingly spoil someone else's pleasure. If your companions think that shrimp or prawn will interfere with their chances of catching salmon, don't fish it.

PART TWO

THE SEA TROUT

CHAPTER 8

INTRODUCING THE SEA TROUT

[HF] The sea trout is a migratory brown trout, although there its likeness to the brown trout ends. It is similar in appearance to the salmon, but has very different habits. And right at the start it is necessary to appreciate that sea trout fly fishing is neither a branch of brown trout nor of salmon fishing. It is a sport entirely of its own.

The slowness of some anglers to appreciate the significance of this was reflected in their approach to sea trout fishing, which resulted in the sport becoming hedged in by convention and occasional absurdities. For instance, almost 70 years ago (when I was a boy, and can well remember) fly fishing 'purists', failing to distinguish between brown trout and sea trout behaviour, and thinking that the canons of brown trout fishing should apply equally to sea trout, regarded people using the Alexandra as being quite beyond the pale!

Like salmon flies, most of the flies used for sea trout fishing are, simply, lures. Few of them, after all, are imitations intended to deceive a feeding fish.

A migratory fish, carrying its rations on its back and having no need of food, does not necessarily take a fly because it is hungry. Almost certainly it has lost its appetite on its return to fresh water and, when it 'takes' most probably does so from force of habit: the feeding habit it has indulged during its recent life at sea and during its earlier life in the river as a parr.

But this was not the popular concept. According to legend, all migratory fish continued to feed on their return from sea; a view that earlier angling writers had done nothing to discourage.

That such a belief should persist into modern times is strange. Quite apart from the observation of sea trout behaviour and examination of their stomach contents after capture, a little thought puts the matter beyond doubt. And a detailed analysis of this will be found worthwhile, for it has considerable bearing on our fly fishing strategy.

Like salmon, the huge numbers of sea trout that run into fresh water each year eat very little for the good reason that there is very little for them to eat. Most of our waters hold only a small proportion of the food that would be necessary to support such vast populations of migratory fish with normal appetites, in addition, of course, to the populations of resident species.

While in salt water sea trout feed greedily and can be caught whilst they are feeding. If they retained their appetites and continued to hunt actively in fresh water, we might expect that the longer they remained in their new and less fertile environment the greater their efforts to find food and so the greater our chances of catching them. But experience proves the opposite. Like salmon, the longer sea trout live in fresh water, whether river or lake, the less interest they show in a food item, or, for that matter, an angler's lure; and, needless to say, the harder they are to catch.

I refer specifically to sea trout with a sea life of one year plus, not to young fish - the herling, whitling, finnock, or what-have-you - a certain number of which undoubtedly continue to feed in fresh water as avidly as the food supply permits and which are usually easy to catch.

By this I do not suggest that the mature fish eats nothing at all. Many adult sea trout swallow food items from time to time when these are available. (So do salmon; more than once I have watched salmon respond to a hatch of fly.) But there is a great difference between the taking of occasional food items and 'feeding'. If 'feeding' is defined as the regular taking of food for the purpose of maintaining life, then, like the returning salmon, most sea trout can, and should, be regarded as non-feeders.

The above section is as Hugh Falkus wrote it. After long discussions with

Hugh, Malcom Greenhalgh has appended the following notes.

What Hugh says is absolutely right as far as the river that he fished for so long is concerned, the little west Cumbrian Esk. But it needs further qualification as far as many other rivers are concerned.

In certain rivers and lakes, and under certain conditions, sea trout will take food (both surface flies and subsurface nymphs) and can be caught by anglers fishing dry fly or nymph. Indeed, I have caught sea trout that were 'feeding' (in the sense of taking every natur-al fly that floated down over their

HF with a fine sea trout caught the previous night

heads) in 26 rivers in Britain and Ireland, and in three Irish loughs. The biggest was 4½lb (that fish had been taking pale watery duns on the Lune); my son Peter hooked and lost one, also on the Lune, well in excess of that size.

I am not talking of individual sea trout, but lots of fish in the beat or pool. For instance, during one August week on the Aberdeenshire Dee Oliver Edwards and I had 22 sea trout on the dry fly; in two hours of a hot July afternoon, when I was demonstrating dry fly fishing for sea trout on the river Mourne, I hooked six fish in seven casts; and in two afternoons on the middle Spey I had 11 sea trout on dry fly.

There is nothing exceptional about this: if conditions are right for dry fly or nymph, then any angler who is prepared can enjoy good sport.

For good dry fly and nymph fishing for sea trout, four conditions must apply:

1. There must be a good head of sea trout (obviously!)....but the fish must not be fresh from the sea. I have never caught a sea-liced fish on dry fly or nymph. They must have been in the river for, perhaps,

101

two or three weeks. I am not talking of catching stale, brown sea trout. Indeed, one ought to avoid these, for they are almost inedible and should be left to spawn. I am talking of sea trout that are still bright silver or, at worst, pewter-silver. The sort of fish caught in the middle Spey during late June and July.

2. The river must be low, the water warm and the weather hot. There is no need to wait until the evening. I have caught many sea trout, on both dry fly and nymph, on sweltering afternoons.

3. The river must produce a good hatch of fly. For dry fly fishing the parr, brown trout (and, in some rivers, grayling) should be feeding. Indeed, by matching-the-hatch, the bag would include all these, together with sea trout. But when I am going to catch sea trout I avoid these lesser fish by not matching-the-hatch precisely.

4. The sea trout can be seen, taking natural flies. Seen? The rise of a two pound sea trout to a natural fly floating on the surface can be a 'spladoosh' that betrays its size. On the other hand, the rise may be the slightest of sips as the fish gently takes the fly. It is more difficult to detect sea trout that are "feeding' on nymphs and larvae deep below the surface, though in many rivers they can be observed from a suitable vantage point. Alternatively, fish the nymph through lies that you know, from night fly-fishing sorties, hold sea trout.

When conditions (1), (2) and (3) apply then I will go with confidence to catch sea trout. If they are taking natural flies at the surface then I fish dry fly to them; if not, nymphs and bugs.

Note: also that, if the river has a good head of recently-run grilse and summer salmon, these too will occasionally take dry fly and nymph. But whereas a sea trout will usually take the dry fly or nymph on the first cast, salmon often need to be pestered and may eventually take on the umpteenth cast.

The question remains, to what extent are these sea trout feeding?

Often the sea trout that I catch on both dry fly and nymph have nothing, or just one or two items in their stomachs. Many times I have watched a sea trout take two or three natural flies, then caught it, and found nothing in its stomach. Such sea trout, I believe, are taking food but not swallowing it. Instead, I think, they are expelling what they have taken via the gills.

By contrast I have caught sea trout that were clearly feeding. The most recent occurrence was in early July on Northern Ireland's river Mourne. Five fish, seen to be taking bluewinged olives and taken on dry fly, had stomachs crammed with flies.

In the former the fish seem to be 'going through the motions': they are taking potential food items but, because they are not ingesting them, they are not really feeding. It is as though, if I may use a little anthropomorphism first used by Arthur Ransome, they are chewing gum. By contrast, some sea trout in some rivers do feed when conditions are appropriate.

What is the consequence of my researches on dry fly and nymph fishing on angling for sea trout?

Firstly, what Hugh discovered in his researches on night fishing is 100% kosher. On all rivers, through much of the season, sea trout tend to take a lure mainly by night (salmon, mainly by day). But secondly, my observations extend (on some rivers and in certain conditions) the opportunities of catching sea trout in the daytime. The use of dry fly and nymph is thus an additional method to try when the river conditions are at their worst and when most anglers leave their rods at home.

Life of the Sea Trout

The early life of the sea trout is so similar to that of the Atlantic salmon that there is little point in dealing with it in great detail. Sufficient to say that, like the salmon, the sea trout is born in fresh water where it spends the first two or three years of its life, going through the stages of alevin, fry and parr, finally assuming a silver coat and, as a smolt, migrating to sea.

The full story of the sea trout's life at sea is not known. It has often been said that sea trout travel little further than their local estuaries, but research indicates that the fish from (at least) some rivers make substantially greater journeys. In his excellent book *Child of the Tides*,

Edward Fahy remarks:

'Scottish investigations of sea trout migration suggest that the fish fan out from their natal river. There are numerous examples of individuals moving in excess of 65 miles (about 100 km) along the coast and some may even travel more than 300 miles (about 500 km).'

Whatever distance it travels, however, the sea trout (like the salmon) goes to sea in order to feed and grow. And while at sea it feeds avidly. Although its tastes are catholic, in many areas its diet consists mainly of small fish: sand-eels, sprats and the fry of herring and mackerel. Also important food items in some areas are shrimps, prawns and small crabs.

In most sea trout rivers the fish begin to run in June or early July, though in others they may start as early as April or May. In some rivers the run may peter out through August, though in many the fish continue to arrive from the sea through September.

Unlike salmon, that usually run the river when water levels are high, sea trout will creep upstream in the lowest of conditions, splashing through the shallowest riffles with their backs out of the water. Rarely do these sea trout move far in one evening. Perhaps through two or three pools and riffles in small streams, or three or four miles in big rivers.

However the biggest arrivals of sea trout occur in the later stages of a spate, especially when these coincide with spring tides. And in the higher water the fish will run far, quickly. Sea-liced sea trout (indicating fast-running fish, for the lice fall off after about five days in fresh water) can be caught many miles upstream of the tideway in the later stages of a spate.

Note: The biggest fish tend to run early and late in the season. These large fish are ideal presents for the bank manager, for the best fish on the table are those weighing between 1½ and 4 lbs.

Sea Trout and Salmon Identification
The main five points of difference are as follows:
1. Tail

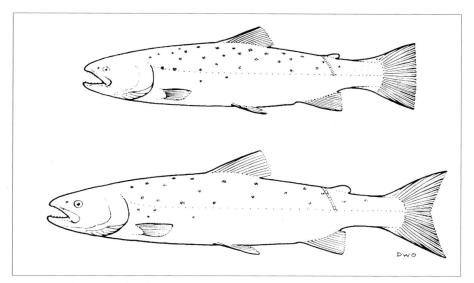

Sea trout (top), and salmon

When relaxed, the tail of a biggish sea trout is square. When stretched it becomes convex. From being forked when relaxed, the salmon's tail straightens out but with two'horns'.

2. Wrist

The base of a salmon's tail (the caudal peduncle) has a pronounced 'wrist'. This enables an angler to tail a salmon. The sea trout's broader-based tail has no wrist. Hence a sea trout cannot be tailed, and should be netted or beached.

3. Scale Count

The scales are counted from the front edge of the adipose fin backwards and downwards to the lateral line.

Sea trout count: 13-16, usually 14

Salmon count: 9-13, usually 11.

4. Anal Fin

With the anal fin closed, the outermost ray of a sea trout's fin is nearest the tail. The innermost ray of the salmon's fin is nearest the tail. The sea trout's upper jaw reaches well past the hind edge of the eye. The

Size has nothing to do with identifying salmon and sea trout. This fish, weighing 2¹/₂ lb, is a salmon.

salmon's upper jaw reaches only to the hind margin of the eye.

The Approach to Sea Trout Fishing

As many anglers have discovered to their cost, sea trout are extremely shy. Their vision is very acute and they are highly sensitive to vibrations, both from movement on the bank and in the water. Frighten one fish and alarm can spread quickly through a shoal, even though other fish in the shoal may be unaware of what has caused the disturbance.

No matter how suitable his tackle and lures, no matter how skillfully he may cast, the angler is doomed if the fish have fled. A sea trout angler must learn to think and act like a hunter. He must know where the sea trout are lying or are likely to be lying. Then it is vital, for success, that the would-be catcher of sea trout keeps out of sight of the fish and moves stealthily. Even at night.

There are anglers who arrive for a night's sea trouting in herds in broad daylight, thunder about against the skyline, and, before it is fully dark, wade in amongst the lies and thrash their lines across water from which every fish has vanished.

There are anglers who seek the company of others whilst they are fishing, and who constantly chatter. Perhaps such anglers are frightened of being alone in the dark. Many are. But although chatter will not disturb the fish, it will certainly affect the fisherman. Nothing destroys concentration so effectively as chatter, and concentration is essential to successful sea trout fishing. Lack of concentration is one of the most common reasons for fishing failure.

Nothing is more off-putting, and infuriating, to other anglers than shining a torch over the river. If you must change a fly, or undo a tangle, leave the water and take refuge behind a bush or dry stone wall. Remember also that torchlight will temporarily spoil your night-vision. After using a torch, wait in the darkness for a few minutes for your night-vision to recover.

The following photographs were taken in daylight on sea trout pools. What they show applies equally to fishing by night.

Incidentally, it is possible to wade very close to sea trout at night provided you move slowly and carefully. By so doing, a shorter cast can be made which allows for better presentation of the fly.

The ideal night for sea trout fishing is one with no moon. *(See diagram overleaf)*. But that occurs on only three or four nights each 28 day lunar cycle. When the moon is between half and full (14 days each lunar cycle) then the angler must consider his position in relation to the moon.

Never fish with the moon behind you. Take up a position that allows you to cast towards the moon, perhaps by crossing the river or changing pools.

This beat (on the following page) has three holding pools, A, B and C. Your permit allows you to fish from the right bank only. The moon will appear above the eastern hills about an hour after dusk. As it appears it will be behind your rod if you are fishing pool C, later it will shine directly down the pool. So start with pool C before moonrise.

As soon as the moon shows above the hills, go immediately to pool A. The trees along the left bank provide some shadow and the moon

If you need to wade, wade deep. The deeper you wade, the less of you sticks up in the air and the less likely you are going to disturb the fish

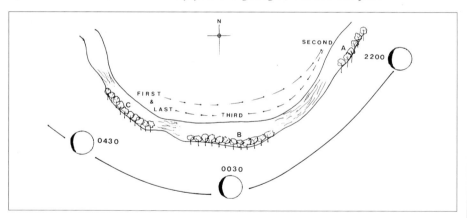

Beating the moon.

is in front of you. The moon is now shining straight down pool A.

Two hours later the moon will have moved around to the south. Now you can fish pool B. Again the trees on the left bank will provide shadow and you will be facing the moon.

Just before dawn the moon will have moved round to the south-

Do not assume the fish are always on the other side of the river. Here the salmon and sea trout lie close in, almost under the bank. In very clear water, kneel down and, if possible, make use of any available cover.

CHAPTER 9

FLY-FISHING FOR SEA TROUT IN RIVERS

Tackle Check List

This check-list is important, for it is all too easy to forget some important item when going out for a night's fishing. Notes on many of the items listed are given with the salmon fishing check-list at the front.

SEA TROUT TACKLE CHECK LIST

Rods. For night fishing: Two, 10-10½ feet in length, taking:
Lines on reels. AFTM DT 7 Floater and Fast Sinker. Also worthwhile carrying a DT 7 Sink-tip or Intermediate line to use instead of the floater in very fast water (although in all rivers the floater is essential for fishing the Surface Lure).
Rod. For nymph and dry fly fishing by day: Although the 10½ ft AFTM 7 rod can be used, it is on the heavy side for daytime fishing. Far better is a 9-9½ foot rod, taking a No.5 or 6 floating line.
Leaders. For floating line fishing at night a level piece of nylon, about 9-10 feet in length, is fine; and for sunk line tactics the same but shorter (about six feet). At night sea trout are not leader-shy: use 12-15 lb BS for Surface Lures and Sunk Lures, 8 lb for Medicine, Secret Weapon and small doubles.
For daytime fishing, a 10-12 foot tapered nylon leader is advisable, with a

point of 5 lb test. For dry flies, nymphs and tiny wet flies.
Fly Boxes
Spare nylon (15 lb, 12 lb, 8 lb, 5 lb)
Wading Staff
Landing-Net
Priest
Waders: Chest and thigh
Scissors or nylon-snips
Artery forceps
Spectacles
Torch (with spare bulb and batteries)
Midge Repellent
Dry-fly flotant
Leader Sink. A paste made by mixing Fuller's earth and washing-up liquid which, when applied, helps sink the leader (essential in dry fly and nymph fishing)
Fish carrier/bass
Maggots. For fishing the Secret Weapon; but check that the fishery rules permit their use.

10'. 6" Fibre glass "New Era"
Sea trout rod. B. James & Son in
association with Bruce & Walker
(fished with this at night for years
fine sea trout rod.)

HF's first fibre glass sea trout rod was eventually pensioned off with this label attached

Night Fishing: the flies and presentation
General Principles

On most rivers there are three main taking periods:
1. From dusk until about midnight (the 'first-half')
2. From about 1.00 until daybreak (the 'second-half')
3. The hour of sunrise ('extra-time')

The period between first-half and second-half is known as 'half-time'. Sport is often slack during this short period, and it is the ideal time to have coffee and prepare tackle for the second-half.

Any angler who packs up at midnight, thinking that the fish have 'gone down' for the night, deprives himself of many chances, not least, the chance of catching a big sea trout. On average, more big sea trout are caught after midnight.

We noted that this pattern applies on 'most rivers'. Anglers fishing the rivers of northern Scotland (including Dee and Spey), where the night is short and, in high summer, never pitch-dark will find that the entire night is 'first-half' in character.

During the first-half sea trout are most active: they will be seen (or more likely heard) splashing about in the pool. Many of these fish will be running fish that have just arrived in the pool or are preparing to move on, for the first-half is the period when most sea trout run the river, especially in low water conditions. Such sea trout will readily take a fly fished close to the surface, and so the angler will do well to fish a 'medicine' type lure on a floating line (in very fast water, a sink-tip or intermediate). It is best fished fairly fast. But since this lure is supposed to simulate a little fish, the angler will be wise to present it at a speed possible for a creature of that size to attain.

Sometimes sea trout remain active all through the night. On these occasions the same fly can be fished to dawn, and an exceptional bag taken. But, save for northern 'twilight' rivers, such nights are rare. A typical night usually starts with a taking period lasting perhaps from 45 minutes to an hour and a half. After this, the fish usually stop taking a fly fished just below the surface, and 'go down'. Quite suddenly the river seems utterly lifeless, the fly swings across the pool untouched, and at this point many anglers lose heart and go home.

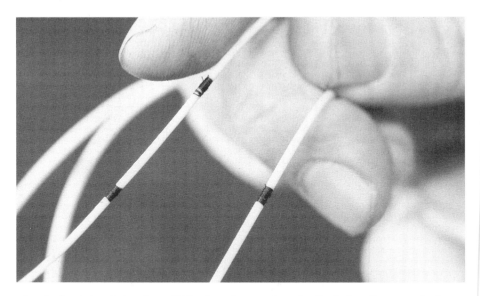

On dark nights it is often difficult to know that the fly is landing precisely against the far bank, under the trees where the sea trout are lying. For certainty, mark the line. Line markers on MG's floating line give the casting range for fishing a favourite pool.

Unless they have to be up early in the morning, they are almost invariably wrong. The fish are certainly down, and the chances are that they will stay down and (with the remarkable exception of the Floating Lure) not be prepared to rise far to take a lure. But if the angler has the recommended lures and presents them correctly he can enjoy opportunities of catching fish throughout the night. He will, however, need to make considerable changes in technique during the second-half.

In the first-half, just one rod was used. At half-time a Surface Lure replaces the Medicine on the floating line.

For reasons unknown, a sea trout that now declines a fly fished just under the surface, or a deeply sunk fly or maggot, will sometimes rise furiously to a lure that is dragged across the surface. It must be dark for the Surface Lure to be effective, and usually this means after midnight, in the second-half.

But in the second-half most sport will come to the second rod, armed with a sinking line and a tandem-hooked Sunk Lure or a fly-maggot combination (ideally, the Secret Weapon) or a wee double.

The aim, with this tackle, is to offer a lure to the fish in such a way that it can be taken with the minimum effort. This means sinking it close to the bottom and getting it to swing round in front of the fish's nose as slowly as possible. On most nights, unless fished for in this manner, very few sea trout will be caught.

It is important that the principles of sunk line fishing are clearly understood. An angler who thinks that it consists merely of sinking the lure is deluding himself. A lure or fly will fish correctly only when its longitudinal axis forms a direct continuation of the leader and line. It is, then, the line that maintains the position of the lure close to the bottom.

The line must be fully sunk. A floating or semi-floating line will prevent the lure from swimming deep on an even keel; it will tend to lift its nose as soon as it is moved.

The use of a weighted lure (e.g. aluminium tube fly) is of value only in a strong current. But where the water is slack it is impossible to fish a heavy lure slowly enough, and it is in the slacker, deeper water that most sunk line fishing is carried out at night. True, the lure must fish deep; but it must also fish slowly without losing its trim. For this reason, a light iron or tandem mount is more effective, fished on fast sinking line, than a heavy lure fished on a lighter line.

Everything relating to fishing the Sunk Lure on a fast sinking line applies equally to fishing the small double, or maggot on a Secret Weapon. Both can be deadly methods of catching sea trout late at night. But the secret is to fish them deep and slow.

At daybreak, when the riverbed becomes clearly visible, the Surface Lure is snipped from the leader and a small Medicine or tiny double tied on in its place. This small fly can be fished well into daylight.

Now in the cool of the morning there is a splendid chance of hooking a salmon ...

Sea Trout Night Flies

With a little practice any angler can soon learn to tie flies that catch fish, provided that he tries to avoid neatness and a polished finish. Like salmon, sea trout prefer something rather drab, straggly and well-chewed. Presentation is all-important. No fly, however famous or well-tied, will live up to its reputation if it is not fished attractively.

There are few rivers without their own special fly patterns which, it is claimed, are essential to success. Sometimes, indeed, they may be, and if the locals catch fish on them, so too should the visitor. But do not regard them as the only flies worth trying. Many local anglers are inclined to be conservative both in their choice of flies and methods of fishing.

The few lures we describe have proved their worth many times on many different rivers. Anyone fishing them properly should seldom experience a blank night.

Since the following flies were first described by HF in his book *Sea Trout Fishing*, both HF (in his latter days) and MG have experimented with the addition of Lureflash Crystal Hair to both salmon and sea trout flies. The addition of three or four strands of this modern material seems to enhance the effectiveness of the lure . Most tackle shops ial seems to enhance the effectiveness of the lure . Most tackle shops sell a wide range of this inexpensive material. Pearl and smolt blue appear to be most useful for sea trout flies. But let us stress: Don't overdo it. No more than three or four strands per lure.

The Medicine

Hook	Sizes 2, 4, 6, Low Water salmon
Thread	red or black
Body	hookshank painted with metallic silver Humbrol paint or similar
Hackle	blue; 2-3 turns
Wing	wigeon, teal or bronze mallard; or the equivalent three 'shades' of natural grey and dyed brown and black squirrel tail.

Plus 3-4 strands pearl Lureflash Crystal Hair.

This is a general purpose fly: good at night in clear water, and during

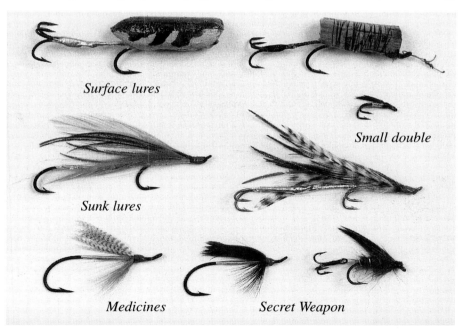

Surface lures

Small double

Sunk lures

Medicines   *Secret Weapon*

Sea trout night-fishing lures

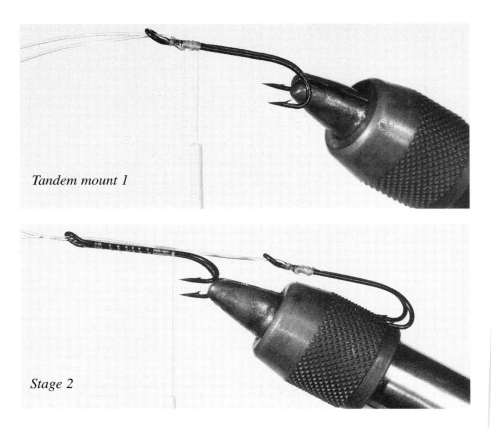

Tandem mount 1

Stage 2

the day when the river is falling from a spate and slightly coloured. It has all the features of a good sea trout fly - simplicity and slimness. The slim-line dressing on a low water hook with a silver-painted shank provides just that.

The Medicine can, of course, be fished effectively all night, provided that both floating and sunk line techniques are used. But, generally speaking, the night fly-fisherman will get better results after midnight by using Sunk Lure, Surface Lure and Secret Weapon, especially if conditions become difficult: a sharp drop in temperature, ground mist, bright starlight, distant thunder etc.

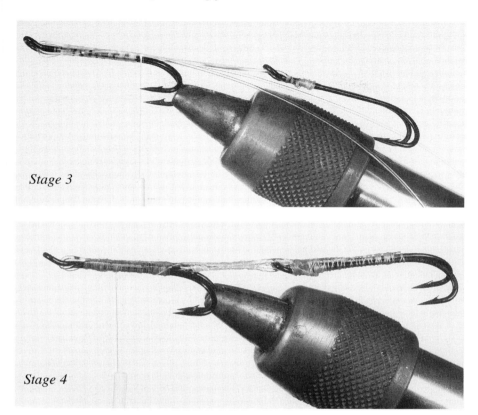

Stage 3

Stage 4

Tandem Mounts

The next three essential flies are dressed on tandem mounts. These are easily made. The following is a modification of HF's method, the modification strengthening the mount and also virtually guaranteeing that both hooks are perfectly in line.

    1. Fix the rear hook in the vice.

    a. Put a seating of tying silk half-way along shank of tail hook.

    b. Loop an 8-10 inch length of nylon round the hook and bring both ends out through the eye. The thickness of the nylon used will depend on the size of the hook and the intended length of the lure. It should be stiff enough to support the tail hook without drooping. For Sunk Lures and Surface Lures: 20 lb BS. For Secret Weapons: 8 lb BS.

Remove the rear hook and attached nylon.

2. Fix the front hook in the vice.

a. Whip thread down the hookshank.

b. Take the rear hook with nylon attached, and pass one of the nylon lengths through the hook eye. Whip down lightly with about six turns of thread. Repeat with the other length of nylon.

c. Now pull on the rear hook or two nylon lengths to give the desired length of mount (see below).

d. Tightly whip the two nylon lengths along the top of the hookshank, leaving one hook-eye diameter of shank free of thread immediately behind the eye.

e. Pull back the ends of the nylon so that they fit snugly into the back of the eye of the front hook and whip the two nylon strands tightly back along the top of the hookshank. Make several extra turns at the rear of the shank of the front hook (this is a weak point) and whip finish.

f. Fix the mount in the vice by the rear hook and carefully whip together, with touching turns, the connecting four strand nylon link between the two hooks. Continue whipping back so that you fix the two ends of the nylon along the shank of the rear hook. Cut away any loose ends, whip finish and the mount is complete.

g. Soak the whippings with thin clear cement three times, allowing time to dry in between coats.

You now have a mount where the breaking strain of the link is about 80lb BS for Sunk Lures and Surface Lures, about 24 lb BS for Secret Weapons. The advantage of the four-strand link between the two hooks is that it is heavy enough to prevent the rear hook drooping, but is still very flexible when a fish takes. And by carefully whipping both 'return' lengths of nylon along the tops of both hookshanks the two hooks should be perfectly in line.

Tie these mounts as follows:

Mount 1. Two single Low Water Salmon hooks, sizes 6-10, with an overall mount length of 2½", 3", 4". For saltwater fishing use stainless steel hooks.

Mount 2. Two double Low Water salmon hooks, sizes 6-10, with an overall mount length of 2", 2½" and 3". This mount tends to swim on a more even keel than the previous one.

Mount 3. A small treble (size 10-12) at the rear and a single Low Water salmon hook (size 6) at the front, with an overall mount length of 2½", 3", 4". This is the best lure for holding salmon, and is the one to use in any river with a good head of salmon and sea trout.

These three mounts are for Sunk Lures. After giving them three coats of varnish, paint with Humbrol metallic silver paint and allow three days to dry.

Mount 4. A treble hook (size 6-8) at the rear and single Low Water salmon hook or trout wet fly hook (size 4-6) at the front, with a gap of 1-1½" between eye of treble and rear of front hook.

This is the mount for Surface Lures.

Mount 5. A small treble hook (size 14-16) at the rear and single trout wet fly hook (size 8-10) at the front. The eye of the treble should be level with the rear of the front hook.

This is the mount for Secret Weapons.

The Sunk Lure

Mounts	1, 2 and 3 (see above)
Thread	red or black
Body	silver paint (see above)
Wing	a blue or grizzle or black cock hackle tied along either side of the mount, with 3-4 strands pearl or smolt blue Crystal hair and 6 strands of peacock herl on top of the mount.

The original blue version is highly successful, though later in the season the black version is perhaps more effective. For saltwater fishing, and as an alternative to the blue version in rivers, the grizzle-winged lure is a great catcher of sea trout.

The Sunk Lure is a lightweight lure, good for both sea trout and salmon. It is an excellent clear-water night flyfishing lure for sea trout of all sizes, and especially good for hooking really big fish. It has accounted for many sea trout over the 10 lb mark in addition to numerous salmon. It is the only lure that will consistently catch salmon late, on very dark nights. Tied on Mount 3 it is also a successful daytime salmon lure for sunk line fishing in spring and autumn.

This lure seldom fails to catch fish. Except on those occasions when the river is in spate and coloured, and provided there is a head of fish in the pools, the night fly-fisherman armed with this lure should experience few blank nights. Its particular merit is to attract fish late on - after midnight - when the fish have 'gone down' and are refusing more conventional flies. Provided the night is dark enough, it will catch fish when the river is crystal clear and at dead summer low; also when the water is running high after successive spates - never good conditions for catching sea trout.

It is important that the Sunk Lure should be fished slowly on a sunk line.

The Surface Lure

Mount   4

Thread   black

Body: trim a wine cork or piece of balsa to the desired shape and size, or cut and plug a length of goose quill. Now whip thread along the shank of the front hook of the mount and then bind the body on top of the shank. Varnish the completed 'fly' body and thread whippings.

Colour is unimportant, but you can paint it if you wish; and add two wings (a couple of grouse or woodcock feathers). These are by no means essential, but they may have the merit of increasing the angler's confidence in the fly.

MG uses an alternative body to produce what he calls the 'Night Muddler'. It exploits the natural buoyancy of deer hair.

Deer hair is spun along the entire shank of the front hook (in Muddler Minnow style) and then clipped to shape, leaving a few strands straggling to the rear. This is much lighter to cast than HF's original cork or balsa bodies.

(Our publisher has discovered an excellent source of Surface Lures. Instead of bothering with balsa, cork, goose quills or deer hair, he orders American bass bugs from a New York tackle dealer: Urban Angler, 118 East 25th St. New York, NY 10010. These bugs are cheap, easy to cast and highly effective.)

On a dark night, no matter how low the river, the drag caused by a floating lure moving across the surface can provide a deadly attraction for sea trout. No night fisherman should ever be without one.

For success the night must be like pitch. A still, warm, cloudy night is best, without moon or stars, but no conditions are hopeless. Provided the night is dark enough (as a rough guide, the wake of the lure should not be visible to the angler) sea trout will take the Surface Lure at any hour. The most likely period, however, is between one and three in the morning. The best places to fish it are unrippled runs, and pools tails where the water flows in a steady glide. All holding water is worth trying so long as the surface is calm enough for the lure to create a wake.

On moonlit nights or in the gloaming of the first half the floating lure is not an effective catcher of fish - but it still has a use. Besides catching sea trout, it can be used to locate shoals of fish and waken them up.

When fishing any river where you are unsure of the precise location of sea trout, try the floating lure. Drag it across the flow and fish will splash at it. If they don't take it, go straight back and try the Sunk Lure over the area. This ploy often does the business.

The technique of fishing the Surface Lure is the antithesis of all customary methods of fly-fishing. Usually an angler is careful to avoid the V-shaped furrow in the water surface, caused by his fly skating. But when fishing at night with the Surface Lure it is precisely this drag that he is trying to create.

Obviously, in order to produce drag, the lure must be kept on the move. If, when fished across a current, the line is allowed to go slack, the lure will begin to drift downstream and drag will cease. Similarly if, in slack water, the angler stops stripping-in line the lure will stay motionless, instantly losing its attraction. It is the wake of the lure, not the lure itself, that attracts fish.

It is not unusual for a fish to follow for some distance and take just as the lure is leaving the water. So fish the lure right to the rod tip.

When fishing down a run or pool tail, cast the lure from A to B1 and then flick out a little more slack. The lure will now drift downstream with the current until, at B2, the slack has been taken up. Now, as the line tightens on the lure, the lure will immediately form a pronounced 'V' and begin to swing round on the arc B2/C. Let it swing round to C, and then work it quickly and steadily towards you at A. Fish may take anywhere as the lure is waking across the surface. Sometimes a fish will make a dash at the lure, just before you are preparing to make the next cast. To encourage any following fish to take boldly, increase the speed of the lure between C and A.

This technique is useful when there is good holding water downstream, beyond casting range or where it is impossible to cast conventionally (for instance, heavily treed runs or pools).

Wade out to A, and let the lure drift downstream along the edge of the current by stripping out line. Work the lure in zig-zags across the stream (see dotted lines in the diagram) by holding the rod at arms length, leading the lure around and controlling the line with the non-rod hand. Try 'hanging' the lure in the strongest parts of the current, lead the lure back and forth over potential lies, let it drop downstream inertly and then 'wake' it back up and across the stream, taking care to fish thoroughly any deep, slack water under overhanging branches.

Strangely, the success of the Surface Lure varies from season to season. Some years it catches a lot of sea trout, in others very few. Even so, it is capable of attracting the biggest fish in the pool on a night when all other methods fail.

The Secret Weapon

Mount	Mount 5
Thread	brown or black
Body	dubbed brown fur or none at all

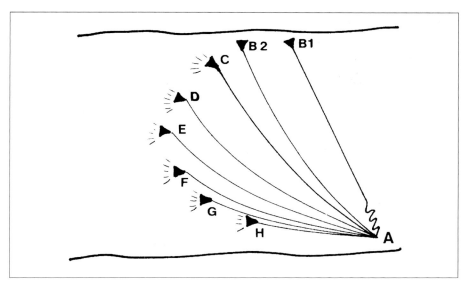

Fishing the Surface Lure

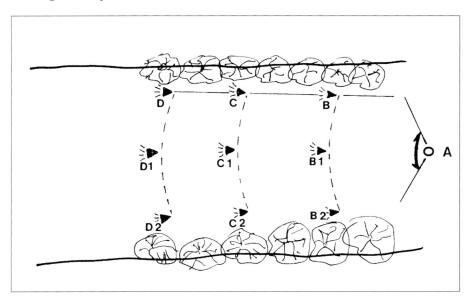

Two-way fishing the Surface Lure

Hackle   fairly long-fibred brown hen, 2-3 turns
Wing   slender, bronze mallard

Note that the wing should extend no further back than the eye of the trailing treble (that, in Mount 5, should be about level with the bend of the shank of the front hook carrying the dressing).

The Secret Weapon was designed to be fished with one or two maggots impaled on the bend of the front, single hook. There are times when the combination of fly and maggot can be a very successful method of catching sea trout at night. Traditionally the lure was a small wet fly tied on a single hook, with one or more maggots attached.

When a sea trout takes with gusto, this arrangement is quite satisfactory since, together with the maggots, the hook is sucked into the fish's mouth. But sea trout do not always take in such an obliging manner. Often, using the very front of the mouth, a fish will give the maggots a little tweak and then let them go again, rather in the same way that a salmon will nip a prawn or shrimp. The maggots come back crushed. Such infuriating behaviour is especially common when rain is imminent, or when the night turns cold in the small hours. A fish behaving like this cannot be hooked on the conventional wet fly because the hook is never inside its mouth. All the angler feels is a series of little tugs. Although he may strike until his arm aches, his only reward is a slack line.

The Secret Weapon puts an end to all this. Now, when the sea trout tweaks at the maggots, it finds itself lip-hooked by the tiny treble lying astern of the main hook.

Fly/maggot fishing often provides good sport late at night during the second-half when the sea trout have 'gone down'. In these conditions fish are not inclined to race about in pursuit of a lure. To ensure the best chance of its being taken, therefore, the Secret Weapon must be placed right in front of their noses. To achieve this it is fished very slowly on a quick-sinking, smooth-shooting fly line.

How slowly? As slowly as possible. Where the bottom of the river is snag-free gravel or sand and the flow negligible, one trick is to cast out and let the line and fly/maggot settle on the bottom. Then the fly-maggot is being fished hard on the bottom, using the fast-sinking line almost as a ledger-weight. Then, every few seconds give the fly a little tweak. Sea trout will often take such a 'legered' fly/maggot fiercely immediately it moves. This is a most effective method in a clear, still river pool.

In slow-flowing deep pools, cast the fly/maggot across the pool and immediately shoot extra line in an upstream mend so that the fly/maggot has plenty of slack to enable it sink quickly. Then, as the fly/maggot begins to come round, keep everything tight, but without retrieving line.

Fishing the Secret Weapon is delicate work and very exciting. To avoid damaging the maggots a special form of casting action should be developed. It is quite impossible to describe this cast, other than to say that it should be as 'soft' as possible, without jerkiness, and without false casting.

When they are in a tweaking mood, fish are likely to be very lightly hooked through the skin of the lip. Great care must be taken when playing them. The tension of the reel should be slackened and the fish handled as though on cotton.

The Small Double

Hook	size 12 or 14 Partridge 02 Double Wilson
Body	silver
Hackle	black hen, thin and straggly
Wing	teal or mallard

This little fly sometimes does well when sea trout are in a tweaking mood and being finicky. It is difficult for a fish to tweak such a tiny fly without being hooked (although some manage to do it!). When the angler has no opportunity or inclination to fish with maggot, the Small Double provides a good alternative to the Secret Weapon.

Fish taking it are usually well hooked.

The Small Double should also be fished, in summer, in fast, streamy water in the evening and, especially, at dawn. It will take sea trout and, in low water, grilse and summer salmon.

Further notes on fly presentation

As we described the flies needed for night sea trout fishing, so we described how each fly should be fished. These further notes provide further suggestions, for although the fly is important, of far greater

Small flies which have achieved big results. Jonathan Williams caught a 10lb sea trout at night on a Devonshire river with the little fly (size 12) top right. The other flies shown have accounted for sea trout up to 8lb.

importance is the way in which the fly is fished.

Speed of the fly and figure-of-eight retrieve

The Medicine (or any other fly just below the surface on a floating, sink-tip or intermediate line) should be fished fairly quickly. In very fast, streamy water the current, acting on the line that has been cast down-and-across the river, will provide that necessary speed, just as it does in conventional salmon fly fishing. However, where the current is slow, it will usually be necessary to impart movement by retrieving line. We 'work' the fly.

The Surface Lure must be fished quickly, so that it creates a strong wake on the water surface. Fishing the Surface lure quickly means that the angler must retrieve line. We 'retrieve' the fly.

The Sunk Lure, Secret Weapon and Small Double are fished slowly on the sinking line. But that does not mean to say that, after casting, the angler does nothing until either a fish hooks itself or the fly needs to be re-cast. It is essential to keep in touch with the fly, and this is achieved by ever so slowly retrieving line. We 'keep in touch' with the fly.

This 'working'of the fly, or 'retrieving' of the fly, or 'keeping in touch with the fly' is best carried out by 'figure-of-eighting'.

Other methods are used, most commonly stripping in line and letting it fall. But at night the slack line usually becomes entangled in undergrowth or, when wading, gets caught around the legs or wading-stick. Furthermore, when stripping in line the angler has far less feel and control over what is happening out there in the darkness, at the end of the leader.

The conventional figure-of-eight is to draw the line straight from the butt ring, but a far better method is shown in the photograph over-leaf. Here the line is drawn not from the butt ring direct, but from a ring made by thumb and forefinger of the rod hand.

Having made a cast, grasp the rod only by the 3rd, 4th and 5th fingers of the rod hand and pass the line over the crook of the index finger. Drop the thumb until it touches the ball of the index finger. Thumb and index finger now perform the role of an extra rod-ring - the thumb-finger ring.

Take hold of the fly-line behind the thumb-finger ring with index finger of the left hand and draw about four inches of line through the thumb-finger ring.

Grab the line with the remaining fingers of the left hand. Allow the loop that has formed over the tip of the left forefinger to slip off into the palm as the hand moves back into its former position.

Repeat the procedure with the wrist pivoting in a smooth figure-of-eight movement. It is important to keep the hands very close together; indeed, the angler should be concious of his left little finger brushing the right thumb with each backward stroke.

Gradually, as the fly is worked in towards the angler, coils of line

The thumb-finger ring figure-of-eight retrieve

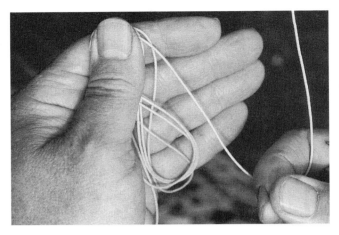

are gathered up in the left hand. The gathered line is shown in with the hand displayed in an open position. This has been done purposely to reveal the coiled line. In practice, the hand merely opens sufficiently to grab each succeeding coil of line.

The advantages of the thumb-finger ring figure-of-eight over the conventional method are:

1. It is much easier to perform.

2. It is faster, thus permitting greater variation of fly speed during recovery. In slow water a Medicine can be fished quickly. A Surface Lure very quickly. And when fishing the Sunk Lure, Secret Weapon or Small Double slowly on a sinking line, a very slow figure-of-eight can be used to keep in touch with the fly and feel, through the thumb-finger ring, the gentlest of offers.

3. When a fish takes, the line is under immediate control. One has simply to exert pressure with the right forefinger and trap the line against the rod butt.

Note: The figure-of-eight retrieve is made much easier if the rod butt is kept firmly anchored against the stomach. For this reason, it is advisable to fish with a rod that has a short extension below the reel.

Fishing Round-the-Clock

In still water (and many excellent sea trout lies are in slackwater pools with no significant flow to work the fly), the cast can be in any direction, but the fly must be worked by the angler otherwise it will sink to the riverbed as an inert, inanimate object. Fishing round-the-clock is the ideal way of fishing these lies.

Fishing round-the-clock can also usefully be employed on slow to moderately fast pools. It not only enables the entire pool to be fished, but means that, as the angler works his way up (preferably) or down a pool, every fish sees the flies approaching from different directions and at different speeds. Often, having seen the fly approach at one speed and from one direction but ignored it, the same fish will take a few minutes later when the same fly approaches from a different direction and at a differnt speed (rather like backing-up).

Fishing round-the-clock is the ideal way for a novice to learn to fish for sea trout at night, for the angler stays in one position whilst several casts are made.

All night fly fishing methods can be used round-the-clock: Surface

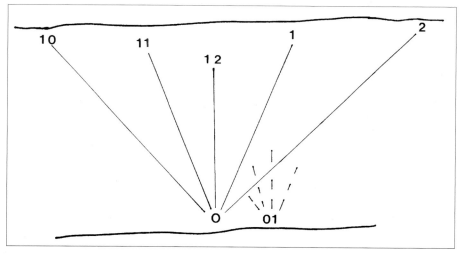

The angler at 0 casts to all holding water 10, 11, 12 1 and 2 o'clock. These casts may be repeated before the angler moves to 01 from where a similar series of round-the-clock casts are made. Often a cast made to a lie fished from the previous position (eg 12 o'clock for the position O which becomes 11 o'clock for position 01) will take a fish.

Fishing a sea trout pool round the clock. The fish lie on the far side where the foam is most concentrated

Lure, Medicine on the floating line, and the Sunk Lure, Secret Weapon and Small Double on the sunk line. However there is another exciting method that is very effective at dusk. In effect, it is a stillwater boat-fishing technique applied to the river.

Make up a leader with one dropper. Tie a Medicine on the leader point, and a hackled lake fly - a Claret Bumble or Zulu will do admirably - on the dropper. Treat the dropper fly with flotant.

Wade carefully into the tail of the pool to a position from which fish can be covered with a fairly short line, and stand perfectly still. Start by casting upstream at an angle of, say, eleven o'clock to the opposite bank. As soon as the flies touch down, draw them in by raising the rod tip and retrieving (with a figure-of-eight). Work them so that the point-fly fishes just below the surface with the bob-fly dragging along on top, leaving a wake. Don't let the flies stop or slow down, but recover in the same smooth movement and cast again. This time from eleven to, say, ten o'clock, and on the next cast nine o'clock, and so on 'round-the-clock'.

If a fish rises but refuses, don't cast over it again too soon. Make several casts well away from it in other directions first.

Having fished several times round-the-clock from the one position, slowly move upstream, casting, every three or four yards, round-the-clock, as you go.

This form of fishing provides the only sensible opportunity of using a dropper at night. Droppers are a curse in the darkness, especially in a gusty wind. But with the short line used for round-the-clock fishing, a bob-fly can be very effective.

Playing and Landing a Sea Trout

Although its flesh hardens rapidly in freshwater, the mouth of a sea trout newly arrived from the sea is very soft. Many fish hooked early in the season are lost, not because they are badly hooked or through any fault of the hook itself, but through this tenderness of the flesh. Normally the best hold is in the scissors at the angle of the jaw. With many early fish hooked in this position, however, pressure on the hook while a fish is being played causes a slit to be torn in the thin flesh at the corner of the mouth. A momentary slackening of the line, especially when a fish jumps, allows the hook to lose its hold. It is said that the hook tears out.

More often than not, however, the chances are that it drops out. Examination of a fish from whose mouth the hook has come away on landing (the fly will be badly entangled in the net mesh) sometimes gives evidence of this.

Unless very fine tackle is being used, or the fish is exceptionally large, it is a good rule when playing a sea trout not to lower the rod point as the fish jumps. Instead, it is better to increase the pressure on the fish as it leaves the water, thus pulling it sideways. This is contrary to the advice usually given on the subject, but any reader who has the confidence to try this ploy will undoubtedly land a higher proportion of early season fish.

If fishing from the bank then it is a simple matter to net or beach the sea trout when they are played out. But when wading it is advisable to net every fish on the spot. As well as avoiding the disturbance of wading to the bank and back again each time a fish is landed, dealing with it on the spot will save time - which is very valuable during those all-too-brief periods when sea trout are really on the take. With a little thought and practice this can be done very easily, provided landing-net, priest and fish-bag are slung ready at hand.

1. When the fish is almost played out, release the net with the non-rod hand and sink it deep. Even in the dark, the bulge of a floating mesh can arouse a fish to make one last surge for freedom. To ensure that the mesh does sink quickly, drop a pebble in the net just before starting to fish. Pull the fish over the sunken net and lift the net to trap the fish.

2. Hold the net handle between your legs and pull some line off the reel. This is to avoid jerking the fly - which is either in the fish's mouth or is entangled in the net.

3. Get the rod out of the way by stuffing the butt down the inside of your waders.

4. Reach for the priest and knock the fish on the head while it is still in the net.

5. Unhook the fish and put the fly out of the way in the rod keeper-ring.

6. Take the fish by the gills, and slip it into the waiting fish-bag.

7. If the fly is tangled in the net slowly untangle it.

8. Re-sling the net.

9. Carefully remove the fly from the keeper-ring, check that the line is running smoothly through the rod-rings, and cast for the next fish.

One word of advice which applies equally to all aspects of night fly fishing for sea trout. Never try to do anything too quickly at night. Every movement, whether we are wading, or changing fly, or landing a fish, should be deliberate and unhurried. Trying to be too hasty in the darkness can waste a considerable amount of time.

Useful Tips for Night Fishing
1. Casting range.
It is difficult to cast precise distance in the dark...to know that your

fly is landing exactly where you want it to land, often within inches of the other bank. A foot too far and you are in the trees. A foot too short and the fly will not cover the fish properly.

A useful tip is to mark your line Two pools and a run are more than enough for one night's fishing, and this may mean that only two or three 'correct' distances need be cast. Go to the river in the morning (the fish will recover from the disturbance by nightfall) and make each cast-distance. At each, when you are casting the perfect distance, whip several turns of thread around the fly line at the butt-ring. Varnish these so that they will not slip. Later, you will feel your markers: the first might be the distance to cast when fishing the narrow run, the second the distance for the little pool, the third the distance for fishing the big pool from the shingle spit. When the markers are level with the butt-ring you know that you are casting the perfect distance.

2. It is very easy to lose things in the dark, especially the second rod. Always carry a large piece of white cloth and use that as a marker (tie it to the tip of rods left leaning against the bank or against trees).

3. Sooner or later we all have to use a torch at night, to unravel a tangle or re-tie a fly. Always do this well away from the water, for light flashing on a sea trout pool will disturb the fish.

It is worth having a special torch for this purpose, one with a dim light that will not ruin your night-vision. Stick a red filter over a conventional torch: you will then be able to do the jobs you need to without ruining your night-vision.

4. Never leave your catch on the bank or anywhere within reach of badgers, mink, otters and other hungry beasts of the night. Suspend fish out of the way (in your fish-bag or on a rope fish-carrier) from tree branches.

5. For the novice, the worst thing about sea trout fishing is being alone, in the dark, with things that go bump in the night. The rasping cough of a roe deer sounds eerily like that of a human. The rattling of shingle as a hedgehog sprints over it can jangle strained nerves. A fox rustling through waterside bracken may sound as though some dread Boggert is approaching.

In time the night fisher learns to take pleasure in sharing the water-side with other creatures. Enjoy their company and the stillness broken only by the breeze sighing in the branches and the sound of running water.

A Swedish Interlude: the Kraefta (Crayfish)

'I was surprised, when I arrived at the Em, to find the black fly was not heard of and Alexandras on a 5 or 6/0 hook were used for the night and evening fishing. When, however, I suggested to Anthony Crossley that he should give it a trial, he was unenthusiastic. At the time he still held the world's record, caught on an Alexandra.

It was in the middle of a kraefta feast when I had partaken of too many crayfish, too much Schnapps and an over-liberal supply of Swedish punch that I sat down at a table to tie a black fly, a fly which I hoped would make the use of the Alexandra obsolete, a fly which I made with unsteady hands, a mind fuddled with alcohol. I selected a Golden Pheasant topping for tail, black mohair for the body, over which I twined some broad, flat, silver tinsel, and with a jet-black hackle and a mixed wing of black dyed-swan and peacock, I put the finishing touches to what the assembled company at once named 'the kraefta'. It was midnight when I finished it and an hour or so afterwards I was scrambling down the steep bank, over great boulders, to Lawson's pool.

It was so dark when I stepped into the water it was impossible to see the opposite bank, though an occasional flash of lightning lit up the scene, vividly picking out the shapes of rocks and trees and, with its attendant thunder, adding a touch of drama to the fishing. In long waders and brandishing a 13 foot rod, I felt more like some will-o'-the-wisp, some spook of the river, than a fisherman about to cast a fly, but overcoming a sudden desire to rush back to bed I flung the kraefta far out into the darkness, to where the water sounded more calm, where any fish fresh from the Baltic should be resting.

For some time I went on casting, methodically, into the black unseen, advancing slowly down the pool. Now I was up to my hips in the water, now standing, perched on a boulder, only my brogues beneath the surface. It must have been during the hour before dawn, when the chances are always best, that the first fish took. I knew he was large as I gaffed him in the light of the torch and carried him to a flat rock. The second fish seemed bigger than the first, but the third I lost. It was much smaller, and, as the line fell slack about my knees, I knew I would catch no more; for the darkness was less intense and, as the dawn broke, I turned towards the bank, pausing for an instant to marvel at the sudden change. Now I could see the other side of the river, see the green meadow and the oak wood behind, the cattle and beyond them the road, while high above the sea eagle was circling, waiting for the sun.

I picked up the two fish and put a rope through their gills; they had served me well. The kraefta had been blooded.

At breakfast, three hours later, Anthony Crossley informed me that both trout weighed over 20lbs, one 25½ lbs, the other 24lbs. He was interested to hear they had taken the black fly, but still sceptical about its value. Gavin Clegg, however, spent the afternoon copying it.

That evening Gavin caught a hen fish of 27lbs, and in the sea pool I landed a cock of 26lbs after a long tussle in the Baltic itself. Both fish took the kraefta.

Late that night Anthony was busy at his vice and by the next evening we were all using the same fly. Within a fortnight Gavin had broken the record with it and thereafter, thanks to my overdose of Schnapps and crayfish, a fly, new to the Em, had become firmly established'.

from *To Be a Fisherman* by Roy Beddington, 1955.

CHAPTER 10

DAYTIME FLY-FISHING
THE FLIES AND PRESENTATION

Through most of the season, on most rivers, the fly-fisher's best chance of catching sea trout will be at night. Most anglers accept this and, if they wish to fish through the day, turn to worm-fishing techniques that will catch both salmon and sea trout without unduly disturbing the water. Nevertheless, there are four situations where fly fishing for sea trout in the daytime can be very effective.

Fishing a spate
There are two periods during a spate when sea trout fly-fishing can be excellent.

The first is just as the river begins to rise following torrential rain (*see* A *overleaf*). Sea trout that have been waiting to move upstream seem to be able to foretell the impending rise of the river, and will begin their journey before the river starts to rise, splashing their way through the shallowest of riffles. Then, as the water begins to rise, these fish will pull in to quiet corners where they will take shelter before continuing on upstream when the spate is subsiding.

These fish readily take the fly through the initial clear-water rise and in the early stages of the ever dirtying flood.

Those fish that are caught will often be quite distinct from the sea trout that have been resident for some time in the pools. The latter may have lost their pristine silver and turned a pewter colour, even quite brown. The fish that are caught at the first lift of a spate are often bright silver, betraying the fact that they had predicted the impending

137

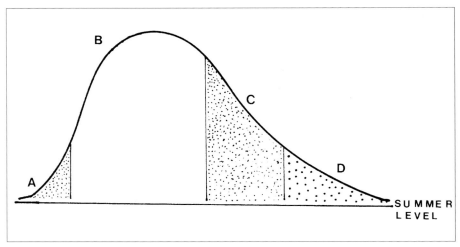

A spate and taking-times

spate and moved into the river before the spate arrived.

As the water continues to rise (B) and turns foul, as the Scots put it, flyfishing ceases to be profitable. Indeed, every cast may reap a mass of detritus purling downstream. Then a worm, fished through quieter corners, gives the best chance of a fish.

The spate eventually begins to subside and, as it does so, then the chances of catching sea trout improve and reach a peak, usually, when the water is still holding colour, but no longer carrying flotsam downstream (C). It is during this latter stage of a spate that a 'magic moment' may occur; when, during a period that may last anything from a few minutes to over an hour, many sea trout may take the fly (D). The precise timing is impossible to predict. The angler should fish hard through the falling spate in the confidence that, sometime soon, a magic moment will arrive. Two or three fishless hours may pass. Then, suddenly, fish after fish will grab the fly. And as suddenly the fish will stop taking: the magic moment will be over.

The spate fly and its presentation
A Medicine or Peter Ross, in sizes 2-8, are ideal spate flies, the smaller sizes (6-8) tied on double hooks.

During a spate, sea trout respond better to a fly that is fished deep, in front of their noses or only slightly above their heads. Thus, in shallow water a sink-tip or intermediate is preferable to a full floating line; where the water is deeper a fast-sinker.

Unless you know precisely where sea trout rest at various stages of a spate, cover as much water as you can during the first-rise or fall of a spate, concentrating on slacker areas out of the turbulent main flow. Cast the fly out, make an upstream mend and, if necessary, shoot extra slack line to help the fly sink, and then fish the fly slowly round. Before making the next cast, do not fail to work the fly back upstream through the slack water under the bank. Often sea trout will lie very close to the bank when resting during a falling spate.

When you do catch a fish, note the exact position for future reference. Some quite small areas are favourite high water sea trout lies - to us, they seem no more attractive than many others that rarely hold fish. But in future spates you can go there knowing that fish will be using that lie.

Indeed, after taking a fish from a particular lie, it may be worth staying put and concentrating on that one lie. Often several fish can be taken in rapid succession from one high water lie during the magic moment.

The low water daytime wet fly and its presentation
To attempt to fish the typical clear-water, slow pools and runs with wet fly during the day is usually a waste of time. Furthermore, the splashing of fly lines on such water and the disturbance caused by a wading angler or a rod flashing in the air, may well reduce prospects for night fly fishing.

However there are some situations where the wet fly fishing can be used without scaring the fish. The first of these is in fast, broken-water pool necks, especially where these are overhung by trees. Because the wet flies will be cast down-and-across the pool neck, it is essential that the angler avoids disturbing the fish. In smaller rivers it may be necessary to approach the water on hands-and-knees, and cast whilst kneeling down. Or to hide behind bankside vegetation.

The second type of water where daytime fly-fishing can be profitable is in the fast, fairly shallow, boulder strewn runs on some of the bigger sea trout rivers, such as the Spey and Aberdeenshire Dee. In hot, low water conditions, sea trout find these fast runs very attractive, possibly because the water is well oxygenated. And to fish a cast of two wet flies, on a fairly long line, through potential lies (in front of or by big boulders, streamy riffles, areas of deeper steadier water close to the bank) can be an enjoyable and profitable way to spend a summer afternoon.

Small wet flies, fished on a floating (in very shallow water), sink-tip or intermediate line are best: Butcher, Connemara Black, Mallard and Claret and Stoat's Tails tied on sizes 14-16 double trout hooks are ideal point flies, with a leader tapering to about 5 lb BS. A second fly can be fished on a dropper: the best dropper fly is the Black Pennell, tied on a size 14 single trout hook.

Dry Fly Fishing for Sea Trout

We have outlined the conditions necessary for good sport with the dry fly and nymph: a good head of fish that have been in the river for some time, warm settled weather and low water, a large natural fly population and, for dry fly fishing, a hatch of flies at the surface.

Usually there seems no need to 'match-the-hatch', for sea trout are not selective 'feeders' as are brown trout. Indeed, where there are lots of parr feeding, it is better to avoid these by deliberately not matching the fly that is hatching.

Instead, use a big dry fly such as a size 8-10 heavily hackled sedge pattern or a big Daddy-long-legs. The lesser fish will almost certainly be feeding on hatching pale watery duns or blue winged olives that are imitated with flies tied on sizes 14-18, and they will ignore the bigger patterns.

Sea trout are not particularly leader shy, so a 9-10 foot leader tapering to 5lb test will do, especially when degreased with leader sinkant. The dry fly is oiled with flotant.

Sea trout dry flies. MG's favourite Sedge pattern (left), which he uses in sizes 8-10. Right, an Irish pattern tied from a recipe found among HF's papers. The body and tail are made from hedgehog belly fur, the hackles fore and aft are black cock. Size 10.

In fast streamy water one can 'fish-the-water' by casting the fly at random. But it is far better to sit down, spot a rising sea trout and then cast to that fish. In flat, smooth flowing water, where the fish are easily disturbed, it is essential to make a careful approach from downstream, and cast to a specific rise.

If a careful approach is made and the fly presented perfectly, the sea trout will usually take the first time it sees the fly. Up it comes ... the fly vanishes in a swirl ... lift the rod and the fish is on.

Having landed your fish, sit down and wait for another to rise. This is a relaxing way of fishing. By being patient and casting only to fish you have seen move at the surface, you may catch a fish every cast. Patience! Two casts per hour resulting in two fish ... but with perhaps 50 minutes of each hour spent watching and waiting.

The dry fly should not drag. It should float down over the head of the fish like a natural fly drifting downstream. Sometimes, where

Fishing the dry fly in a pool neck. During hot weather sea trout rest either side of the main flow. The angler approaches from downstream using a light line and a long tapered leader.

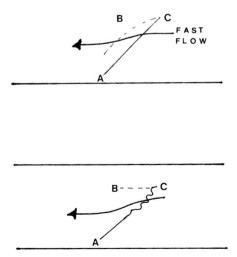

The slack-line cast. Cast straight across fast water (top). The fly will drag as the line is pulled into a downstream curve by the flow. The slack line cast (below) retards drag.

there is fast water between the angler and the fish, the problem of drag arises. In these circumstances the slack line cast is useful.

a) The angler is at A, the fish at B and the fly is cast upstream of the fish to C. However the band of fast water between angler and fish causes the fly to drag before it reaches B.

b) On the next cast the angler at A casts to C, but this time, as the line is extending out over the water, he shoots extra line and, at the same time, quickly waggles the rod tip from side to side several times. The fly lands at C, but the extra line and curves caused by the movement of the rod tip, puts slack line between A and C. The fly now floats down passively to B (where the fish takes the fly), for the line curves prevent the band of fast water putting a tight belly in the line and causing the fly to skate.

Of course, it takes some practice in learning exactly how much extra line must be shot, and how much the rod tip must be waggled, in order to land the fly accurately at C. But once mastered, the slack-line cast will be found invaluable in all types of dry fly fishing.

Some Historic Dry Fly Experiments
Seventy-five years ago, the still unrecognised genius of British fly-fishers, J.C.Mottram, published his account of experiments with sea trout, from which these notes on dry fly fishing are taken. (*Sea Trout and Other Fishing Studies, 1923*). MG does not entirely agree with what Jim Mottram says about drag. This corner of dry fly fishing provides room for further investigation. Here is Mottram's piece:

"In streams where there is an abundance of natural flies, sea trout may be found rising to the natural insects, in which case the best fly to use would no doubt be an imitation of the natural. Where I have fished for sea trout, flies have not been abundant and were never found in their stomachs, although shrimps and nymphs of the Ephemeroptera were often observed in both the stomach and intestine. When, as is usual, sea trout are not rising to natural insects, the question arises-which is the best fly to use? A great number of flies have been tried, and from these numerous tests knowledge has been gained,

143

so that this question can now be satisfactorily answered.

1. Sea trout prefer a fly which floats lightly. For this reason the fly should be tied on a light hook, provided the water be free from weeds and snags. A stiff hackle should be used, rather long in the fibre. The fly should be built of light materials, and, so far as possible, entirely of feathers. Bodies of wool or silk should be avoided, as they tend to become wet and make the fly heavy. In large sizes the hackle should be continued down the body, sparsely so as not to conceal the under-dressing. Wings may often be omitted, or, if required, hackle points should be employed; short wings, as in the 'Variant', may be used, but heavy wings should be avoided.

2. The fish like a fly which floats buoyantly. They take little notice of the fly when semi-submerged, so that materials which become sodden must for this reason also never be used. Unstripped quills, herls and picked fur make the best bodies. Special care should be taken to waterproof the fly.

3. The fish like a fly which drags without being submerged, and which does not leave a large wake behind it.

For this purpose rather long hackles are an advantage. The gut must be oiled right up to the fly. When fishing rippled water a dragged fly should skip from wave to wave, or pass through the wave crest like a silvery ball, and emerge dry at the far side. Such behaviour of the fly is especially attractive to the fish and occurs most often with flies hackled down the body.

4. During the daytime the fish prefer a slimly built fly. An unstripped quill body or one of short ostrich herl gives good results. A stripped quill makes too thin a body.

5. During the daytime the fish prefer a small fly. Sea trout seldom rise more than once to a dry fly, or if they do rise a second or third time, it is very rare for them to be hooked. Having risen a fish, the best chance is to change to a much smaller fly. As a result of these conclusions the following two tyings for flies to be used during the daylight have been evolved:

a) The black variant: body, black ostrich herl: wings, short brown fibres from the tail of the English partridge tied in on either side like the points of a camel hair brush; two or three turns of black ostrich herl in front of the wings; hackle, long glossy black continued down the body.

b) The red gnat: body, unstripped condor quill; wing, the tip of a secondary feather from the wing of a thrush or sparrow, tied in horizontally over the body: in front of the wing, two or three turns of black ostrich herl; hackle, glossy, red, rather long, not continued down the body but placed in front of the horizontal wing.

These flies should range in size from No 17 to No 8; the smallest should be chiefly of the black variant and the largest of the red gnat. A light hook is an absolute necessity if the best results are to be obtained."

J.C. Mottram's dry flies tied by MG. Left: the Black Variant; right: the Red Gnat

Presenting the leaded nymph

Nymph Fishing for Sea Trout

When conditions seem right and the sea trout are not moving at the surface, fishing a leaded nymph is a very effective method.

It is essential to know where the fish are lying or likely to be lying. In clear water a bout of careful watching from vantage points will help. In waters where it is difficult to spot fish, then experience from night fishing should have revealed the main lies.

It is essential that the weighted nymph reaches the bottom quickly, so that it drifts past the nose of the sea trout, not several feet above them. To help with this a longer leader than that used in dry fly fishing is needed: 12-14 feet, tapering to a 5 lb point. And to help the leader sink, before casting treat it with sinkant and re-treat it at the first sign of the nylon floating.

The term 'nymph' is something of a misnomer, for the ideal leaded flies for daytime sea trout fishing are general purpose 'bugs'. They do not imitate mayfly and stonefly nymphs, but are scruffy things that look as though they might be good to eat. And although many reasonable patterns can be purchased, the best are homemade.

The Hare's Ear Goldhead is MG's first choice of 'nymph' for sea trout (and salmon). The French fly-fisher Raymond Rocher, who often fished with the 'nymph pioneer' Frank Sawyer, recommended another ... the Phaisan et Orange. This pattern has a heavy copper wire underbody, orange floss overbody, and tail and back from a cock pheasant tail.

1. Take some size 8-10 wet fly hooks and some 3mm and 4mm 'gold-heads. Goldheads are drilled, gold-plated brass beads, so they add weight and flash to the bug. Slide the goldhead over the hook point and to the eye of the hook.

2. Add extra weight to some, by winding lead wire down the hook-shank. These super-heavies will be used in deeper or faster water.

3. Now take some fur: hare's ear and mask mixed, olive seal fur mixed with a pinch of orange, grey rabbit and hare's ear mixed. Anything that you fancy looks 'buggy'. Dub this scruffily along the hookshank behind the goldhead and rib this body with oval gold tinsel. Add a bit of extra dubbing behind the goldhead (to trap the goldhead at the hook-eye), and tie off.

The tip of the fly line will be bite-indicator, so grease that with mucilin before you start fishing .

The faster or deeper the water, the further upstream of the lie must the bug be cast. In a moderate flow, three feet deep, perhaps six feet, but in a faster flow nine feet or more. Of course in a faster flow one can also gain depth by using a Goldhead with a lead wire underbody. Experience, allied to experiment, is the only way to learn whether to use superheavy or ordinary Goldhead, and how far upstream of the fly should be cast.

If, as the bug comes downstream, the floating tip of the fly line stops, twitches, moves to one side, dips under, or does anything other than carry on drifting downstream, TIGHTEN IMMEDIATELY. And then play the fish.

Wait a second, and the fish will have ejected the bug. TIGHTEN IMMEDIATELY!

Note that both dry fly and leaded nymph fishing as described for catching sea trout also account for numbers of summer salmon every year. Great fun!

A salmon taken by Raymond Rocher on the Phaisan et Orange nymph at Leckford (River Test)), 20 August 1979.

CHAPTER 11

LAKE FISHING

'Let the angler devote the time and study to the loch that has been, and is still being, given to the river, and he will soon discover that it thoroughly deserves and amply repays all attention.'
R.C. Bridgett, *Loch Fishing in Theory and Practice*, 1924

Loch fishing with a team of wet flies or with a dapped dry fly has a long tradition. The lochs of NW Scotland and the Irish loughs provide a splendid variety of opportunities for the visiting angler.

Weather conditions are all important. During a long drought when the river between lake and sea is low, most fish will remain at sea. With the coming of rain, within a few hours of a spate, the fish will be in the lake and in a taking mood. Even during a drought a few sea trout may sneak through to the lake.

Weather conditions play a crucial part in fly-fishing on the lochs. A good wave is what the angler hopes to see, with sky overcast or cloudy and none too bright. A light ripple may be enough but a flat calm and sunshine make fly fishing a pretty hopeless exercise, though a few sea trout may fall to the dry fly at dusk.

Tackle for lake fishing
A long single-handed rod (about 11 ft) taking an AFTM 6 double taper line is ideal for salmon, sea trout and brown trout fishing. A long rod is more effective than a short one in dibbling the bob-fly (see below) on the retrieve.

A double taper line, because most casting from a boat involves roll casting. This is by far the safest method because the flies never cross the boat (as with overhead casting). Overhead casting, especially in a fair wind, can be dangerous.

Roll casting is easy from a boat, down or down-and-across the wind. The other point to remember is that long casting is not necessary, 15 or 20 yards being a very long cast.

In lakes, hooked sea trout and salmon tend not to make very long runs, especially if they are played out in deeper water. Instead of running a long way they usually go deep, swimming in circles. Thus a 3½" wide drum trout reel is adequate, taking the fly line and 100 yards of backing.

We use tapered monofilament leaders in two lengths, nine and 12 feet (the shorter one for strong winds and a big wave) tapering to a point of 7½ lb test.

It is usual to fish with more than one fly on the leader. Two flies are better than three. The point fly is tied to the end of the leader and a bob fly to a dropper tied ideally about five feet up the leader from the point. The dropper of 7lb monofilament is tied to the leader by a water knot. Start with a dropper of about six inches in length.

Lake flies

There is a huge number of traditional fly patterns available for still-water fishing.

Having fished a large number of lakes in both Ireland and Scotland, we offer the following list of proven flies. Choose from these. Yet never disregard the advice of your boatman-gillie. He is on the water day in and day out and knows the whims of the fish on his lake better than anyone.

Point (or Tail) Flies

Scottish Lochs	*Irish Loughs*
Butcher	Connemara Black
Bloody Butcher	Kingsmill
Kingfisher Butcher	Mallard & Claret
Peter Ross	Thunder & Lightning
Teal, Blue & Silver	Silver Doctor

Alexandra
Dunkeld
Cinnamon & Gold
Invicta
Grouse & Claret

Butcher
Cinnamon & Gold
Fiery Brown

Bob Flies

Zulu
Blue Zulu
Black Pennell
Claret Pennell
Bibio
Goat's Toe*
Ransome's Elverine Fly**

Claret Bumble
Bruiser
Grey Ghost
Silver Blue Bumble
Golden Olive Bumble
Bibio
Claret Dabbler

*Some use this excellent lake fly also as point fly
**A useful bob fly for salmon

Sea trout flies for the lake. Top left, Claret Bumble style. Top right and bottom left, tail flies Connemara Black and Mallard and Claret. Bottom right, Olive Bumble.

General boat tackle
1. A large net is essential.
2. A day sitting on a hard seat results in a very sore bum. The ideal boat seat is an inflated small inner tube. This also doubles as a life-buoy .
3. Other tackle items are as for sea trout fishing on rivers.
Warning!

Many reservoir anglers are accustomed to using a drogue to slow the drifting boat. NEVER TAKE A DROGUE ONTO A SALMON OR SEA TROUT LOCH. You will be fishing fairly shallow water, almost certainly where rocks may be just below the surface, often in windy conditions. If a drogue snags a rock it could well capsize the boat.

Fishing a Drift with a Wet Fly
Fishing a drift, or what English anglers refer to as 'loch-style fishing', is one of the most exciting ways of fishing a Scottish loch or an Irish lough. It is also a simple technique. However, fishing a drift is a mis-nomer, for, as we shall see in a moment, the boat should not be sim-ply allowed to drift in a straight line, down wind.

The two greatest problems facing the newcomer to boat fishing are locating the fish and controlling the drifts. No matter how good your flies or your casts, if the boat is drifting out of control in 'dead' water you won't catch much.

Gillies and Boatmen

On the big lakes of Ireland and Scotland it is advisable to hire a boat-man or gillie. Preferably one who has grown up on the lake and knows it intimately in all its moods. The cost may seem high but there will be two of you to share the gillie's wage and the hire of his boat. After a few day's afloat with a good gillie you will have been taught the best drifts, how to control the boat, the best flies to use and how to fish them.

The Fishing Boat Partner

Once you know a lake, its dangers and its lies, then by all means go

Rossinver Bay, Lough Melvin. A spring salmon has taken the fly.

afloat yourself (with an angling friend). Most anglers free-drift in straight lines, directly downwind. But this is the most inefficient way of going about it.

Better to take turns at the oars. On the first drift one takes the oars and manoeuvres the boat carefully, to and fro across the wind (that is slowly drifting the boat in just one direction, i.e. down wind) so that the other angler is constantly covering the best lies. When a hot spot is reached, the boat is held in position so that the other can make several casts. Or it can be brought up and across the wind so that every likely spot is covered properly. If a fish moves at the surface, a couple of pulls on the oar brings the angler's flies over it. Then, when that drift has been thoroughly fished, swap places.

The map shows part of an Irish sea trout lough, with the five and 10ft contours and, shaded, the main sea trout lies. Notice that the main lies are in very shallow water: on a bright day you can clearly see boulders on the lake bed and, occasionally, the boat will bump against them. To prevent damage to the propeller, the outboard should be raised. And to reduce disturbance, the anglers should keep low in the

153

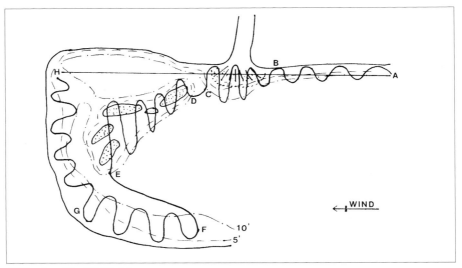

Effective 'Drift' Fishing

boat and not bang about on the keel timbers.

Many anglers row the boat upwind to position A, and then let the wind drift them in a straight line to H. However, for at least 90% of the time they are covering fishless water.

Far better to manoeuvre the boat zigzag along the shore margins A-B, then through the gravel-fan off the inflowing stream B-C, then out (over fishless ground) to fish the skerries D-E, before rowing through deeper fishless water to the shore at F. The boat is then controlled on the oars as it drifts the narrow margin F-G, and is rowed in a zig zag course through the wide offshore shallows to H. On such a route the anglers are covering fish-holding water for at least 95% of the time.

Presenting and fishing the flies from a drifting boat

You are now at the head of a 'drift'. You have a floating fly line on your long loch rod, and at the end of the line a leader carrying two lake flies. You are on the right side of the boat, as it is manoeuvred, side-on with the wind, and your friend is on the left side. You can cast, with due regard to your friend, over an approximately 90° arc, from direct-

Never neglect the mouth of an inflowing stream. Shoals of salmon lie off the mouth of this little river flowing into Lough Melvin. Indeed, just after this photograph was taken, three fish leapt close to the boat lying just off the river mouth, in about three feet of water.

ly downwind round to directly across wind (to your right). Where do you cast within this arc? And do you cast a long line (15 yards or more) or a short line (of up to 10 yards)?

Short-lining

Fish have little fear of drifting boats. On numerous occasions both sea trout and salmon have taken our flies within one yard of the boat and several times when we have been dangling our flies over the side and wondering whether to change flies or tactics. Shortlining takes advantage of this boldness.

Cast about three rod-lengths of fly line down wind, with the rod point finishing low over the water. Wait a few seconds for the point fly to sink. Then pull in any slack line and at the same time slowly raise the rod so that the flies are brought towards the boat (a little faster than the rate of drift). You will (or should) see the top-dropper bob-fly cutting a wake through the surface during this part of the retrieve. Now, with the flies close to the side of the boat, pull in line and keep the rod high so that the bob-fly skitters and bobs on the surface and the point fly is making a wake in the surface film. If a fish does not rise, simply roll cast the flies out, shooting the loose line. Should a fish take at any time, lift the rod point firmly and simultaneously pull the line that is held in the left (non-rod hand) down to set the hook.

Short-lining is one continuous smooth process: cast, raise the rod and pull in some line to make the bob-fly work, dibble the bob-fly, re-cast. And if you can Spey cast (roll cast with a change of direction) it is possible to fish round the entire 90° arc quickly, efficiently and without having your flies or line tangling with your boat partner's or catching him or the boatman in the flesh.

Long-lining

Long-lining is often considered to be exactly the same as short-lining, but with longer casts. Simply cast out a long line, hold the rod low over the water, and pull in line at least a little faster than the boat is moving (to impart life to the flies). Then, as the flies come closer, raise the rod to dibble the bob-fly in the surface film at the side of the boat before making the next cast.

An often more effective method is the 'S' cast and retrieve. Cast the flies on a long line across the wind, at right angles to the line of drift. Aim high and do not be too forceful in the final forward flick. The fly line line will land on the water with the leader and flies curved around in a down wind direction.

Immediately, throw a down-wind mend in the line close to the boat (Do NOT disturb the end of the line or leader).

The line and leader are now on the water in an S-shaped curve.

Hold the rod point low and pull in line. Because of the S-shaped line arrangement, when you retrieve by pulling in line, the flies do not travel in a straight line back towards the rod tip, but in an S-shaped route. As the flies come close to the boat, speed up the retrieve by raising the rod tip and stripping in more line. Then, before making the next cast, dibble the bob fly on the surface.

Sometimes the catch rate between straight long-lining and the 'S' cast and retrieve are insignificant. But at other times the 'S' cast and retrieve greatly outscore the straight line method.

But what happens if you see a sea trout or salmon move at the surface?

It is then imperative that you cover that fish as quickly as possible. This may be difficult. If short-lining, you may need extra line to reach the target area. It pays to be prepared by having a reserve arranged in careful coils on the bottom of the boat or in a line tray. Then it is simply a matter of gauging distance and a quick delivery. Within a second - or two at most - your flies should be in the ring of the rise.

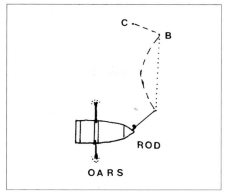

The Long Line S-cast.

If you are long-lining, you will already have sufficient line off the reel. Immediately you see a rise, quickly pull in sufficient line so that you can deliver the flies into the ring of the rise.

The man on the oars can help, for with a few pulls he can position the boat close to the rise and, at the same time, hold the boat against the wind so that it remains stationary.

And as soon as your flies touch down, work them back towards the boat by stripping in line. If the fish does not take, re-cast beyond where you saw the rise and retrieve the flies through the rise position.

Often, a fish that has risen will take the fly immediately.

Dapping

Dapping is one of the most ancient methods of fly fishing wild lakes. It is also the most relaxing. And, some argue, the most boring.

Dapping tackle

Seventeen foot telescopic dapping rods are available on the market; they can be set up in the bottom of the boat, with dapping floss, leader and fly, and reel fixed in place.

However, the most convenient tool is a 15 foot salmon fly rod.

The man on the oars makes a vital contribution to angling success when fishing loch style.

A 15 yard length of dapping floss is attached to a reel line containing about 100 yards of backing and, to the end of the dapping floss a six feet monofilament leader of 10 pound test and whatever dapping fly you fancy. Fished from the drifting boat, the line billows downwind. By manipulating the rod, the fly is put down lightly on the water, lifts off and again touches down.

Dapping flies

Dapping flies are large bushy lures. The aim is to have something unsinkable that can be fished, with a long rod and light floss line, skipping across the water surface from wave to wave. Lightness and action in dapping flies comes from winding many cock hackles in touching turns down all or part of the hookshank, supported by tails and sometimes wings often of bunches of hairs from the squirrel tail. Colour in dapping flies seems to be unimportant: action on the water counts for more. Choose three or four of the patterns given below, tie them in a range of sizes, and you have all the dapping flies you will need on any sea trout or salmon loch:

Badger and Red	Brown Squirrel
Bivisible	Cock Robin
Black and White Dap	Loch Ordie*
Black Pennell Dap	Trivisible
Blue Bird	Yellow and Black Dap

*Besides being tied on the usual large single hook, this very popular dap is also tied on short tandem hook mounts. Some fly dressers also tie in a 'flying treble': a small treble hook tied to a short length of strong monofilament attached to the side of the eye of the front hook. The aim, in both tandem and flying treble mounts is to enhance the hooking power of the lure.

Dapping is a passive pastime. Some anglers find it boring. Others are habitual dappers even in calm conditions. Personally we use the technique as a break from the repetitive casting of a team of wet flies. It is a relaxing way to spend an hour. But when conditions are right for dapping they are perfect for the often more effective wet fly techniques.

It is important not to react too quickly when a fish takes the dap. Time must be allowed for the fish to turn down with the fly. Strike too soon, and the fly will be pulled away from the fish. Some have recommended the angler to shout, 'God save the Queen!' before tightening.

Some of our readers may wish to dap with live insects, a technique which takes us back to the primeval days of fly fishing. Ireland is the home of this primitive method. Grasshoppers and Daddy long-legs are used. As HF put it in another context, 'This method of fly-fishing will not be received with acclaim by all members of the fraternity.'

CHAPTER 12

SALTWATER FISHING

The vastness of the Baltic. At a hot spot on the Danish coast a big sea trout is hooked and running.

Locating the fish

Sea trout smolts go to sea to feed. Therefore, the logical place to fish for feeding sea trout is in the sea. However, location of feeding sea trout in coastal waters is difficult, and takes much time and effort.

Some holding areas are well known: the voes of Shetland and storm-beaches of the Hebrides were once great venues, though in recent years, with the advent of salmon-farms and infestations of sea lice, sea trout populations around many of these islands have collapsed. On some Irish estuaries, such as the Moy, you can charter a boat for a day's fishing. And while Donegal may be best known for its lochs and streams, there are many rock-girt sea-bays along its shores where the sea trout rarely see an angler's lure. Across the North Sea, the coast of Denmark provides excellent sea trout fishing if you can find out the best places.

However the surface is barely scratched! There are many bays and estuaries where the potential for sea trout fishing has yet to be discovered. And not only areas that are close to the rivers run by sea trout. At least one inlet on the Norfolk coast has feeding sea trout many miles from their natal river.

So how does the angler set about the problem of locating feeding sea trout?

First of all, by hard work! In the late 1960s and 1970s MG spent hundreds of hours scouring Morecambe Bay and the Lune, Wyre and Ribble estuaries and located three places where sea trout could be regularly caught. And in the vastness of the Firth of Forth, a hard week's reconnaissance revealed just one site (that yielded 17 sea trout in two tides).

Yet such an effort is usually rewarded, if not by sea trout, by bass, mackerel, pollack, flounders and the occasional mullet. All of them delicious on the table.

There are clues as to the location of potentially good sea trout feeding grounds:

First, there must be a food source: in tidal waters sea trout feed mostly on sand-eels, sprats, small herrings and other fry and on crabs, prawns and shrimps. Where there are populations of these, then there are likely to be sea trout.

The precise location of fish can often be pinpointed by watching sea birds that also feed on lesser fish and crustaceans. The Forth site mentioned earlier was located when MG spotted hundreds of terns plunge-diving for small fish that were being chased to the surface by the feeding sea trout.

Sometimes feeding sea trout are easy to spot. In one Donegal inlet, they were seen leaping clear of the water. That inlet has produced fish of over four pounds: big sea trout by Irish standards. And in other clear-water Irish and Scottish bays and estuaries, sea trout have been sighted moving in with the flood tide and out with the ebb, hunting amongst the bladder-wrack.

But beware of the mullet: the fool's sea trout. Many times we have watched the big, grey forms of mullet follow the flooding tide up estuaries and bays, assumed that they were sea trout, and spent a wasted hour trying to catch them on sea trout flies and spinners. Mullet feed by sucking the tiniest of crustaceans from the mud and rocks, and they will ignore bigger lures. If you want to catch them, try float-fished bread flake or tiny leaded nymphs on very fine tackle. Our publisher caught a fine 5lb specimen at low tide in the Ravenglass estuary fishing 'upstream seaweed': a size 16 treble with an inch of green mohair lashed on. Great sport....but not sea trouting!

Sea Trout Feeding Regime
Sea trout do not feed for 24 hours a day. Their feeding regime is closely linked to the tide cycle.

Where tidal range is great (as in parts of the British Isles) small fish and crustaceans move over the intertidal zone of mudflat, sandflat and rocky shore as the tide floods and retreat on the ebb. So too do the sea trout. In such places you will catch them close to the water's edge, at the head of the flooding or ebbing tide as they chase their prey amongst beds of bladderwrack and kelp, or in the sandy foam of breaking waves.

Timing is critical. In most places, by day or night, the last half of the flood and first half of the ebb is the best period (but excluding a dead half hour or so when the tide is slack at high water). But observations suggest that sea trout are crepuscular by choice, feeding most avidly when high water coincides with dawn and dusk. However, they will still feed on spring tides (those that have the biggest tidal range, that occur on days around full and new moons), even when they occur during the day. Night tides usually produce more fish than day tides (by a ratio of about 3:1). So it is essential to obtain a set of tide tables (from fishing tackle shops or ship's-chandlers at sea ports). These will give you times of high and low water, tidal range and, often, sun rise and set for every day of the year, together with dates of new and full moon. By using these tables you can work out which are likely to be the best tides and days during the year and plan your fishing months ahead.

It is also important to study the places that you are going to fish. Firstly from the point-of-view of safety. Each year sea anglers become stranded by a flooding tide because they have failed to work out a route of retreat. Some are drowned. Make sure that, as you fish the tide up, there is no chance of becoming stranded at the foot of a cliff, or being marooned by incoming waters, or by a flood tide surging up an estuary channel. You need also to work out the route taken by the shoals of feeding sea trout. Often this is quite simple, but in more complex estuaries the shoals may move a considerable distance with the tide and be within casting range for only a few minutes of any tide cycle.

Where tidal range is very small the solar cycle becomes overriding. Whilst it is true that sea trout can be caught throughout the day in estuaries with just a slight tidal rise and fall, the best times are around dawn and dusk, especially when they coincide with high water: concentrate the major effort in the periods two hours before to two hours after sunrise and two hours before to three hours after sunset.

'Few people who fish really understand much about tides and how they can affect angler success. Thus an angler not familiar with a specific area should either hire a guide or at least inform himself about tidal effects on local waters. One of the major reasons why knowing about tides is vital to fishing success is to also understand the baitfish that the predator fish feed on. Unlike many saltwater species, baitfish don't have a home. They may be here today and gone tomorrow. They don't fight tidal currents. Rather, they allow the tide to take them along. Predator species know this and ambush the baitfish in places where the tide will make them available.'

from *Fly-fishing in Salt Water* by Lefty Kreh

So, at low water, sea trout tend not to feed. But as the tide floods, so they will move up an estuary channel or along a bay, seeking prey that itself is moving in search of food. At the high water slack, sea trout usually stop feeding. But then, on the ebb, feeding intensity peaks as they hunt prey that is being carried down the estuary or the coast.

Sea trout feeding in an estuary, see next page. Beginning about two hours after low water, as the tide begins to flow, the sea trout shoals slowly work up the estuary, stopping to feed for periods varying from about 10 to 20 minutes by sandbanks that have recently been flooded (hotspots marked X and numbered in order of the fishes' appearance). For between half and one hour the fish cease feeding at high water, but then drop back through the estuary, feeding at hotspots marked Y. The bank-fisher in this estuary is at a disadvantage, for, even if he fishes one of the best hot-spots (e.g. at Z), he will have feeding fish in front of him for only about ten minutes of the flood and fifteen minutes on the ebb. A boat is essential, together with detailed knowledge of the sea trout feeding regime, to fish effectively throughout the tide cycle.

HF fishing the fly 'round the clock' in a weedy Donegal bay

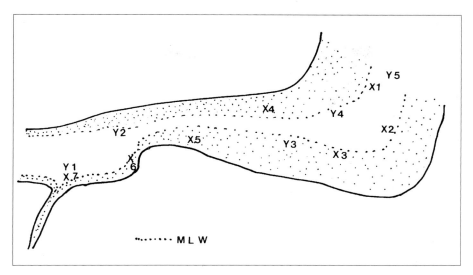

The feeding pattern of sea trout in one large estuary

Dawn on the estuary. A sea trout has taken a fly at position X7 (top).

(a) In this estuary, at the head of an inlet the fish begin to feed 1½ hours before high water and, except for a 15-30 minutes lull at high water, continue to feed for about another two hours until the tide has completely ebbed. Throughout this feeding period, an angler at (A) may enjoy sport for several hours.

(b) In this small bay the sea trout move along the shore in search of food as the tide rises and falls, keeping in water between three and four feet in depth (in other words, they work up the recently covered beach on the flood and retreat on the ebb). Here the wading angler, who works up the shore as the tide advances (A-B) and then follows the ebb down the shore (B-A), will cover any sea trout shoals as they swim past.

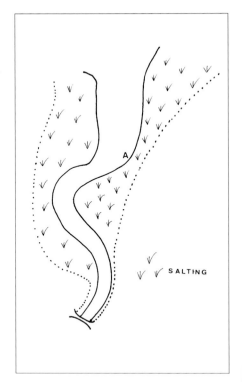

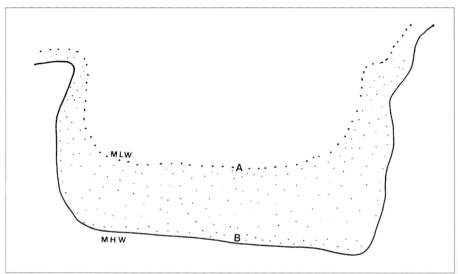

Saltwater Fishing Tackle, Flies, Lures and Baits

For fly-fishing, a matched pair of 10-10½ foot fly rods taking AFTM seven lines. The first rod carries a floating, intermediate or sink tip line: Use this outfit if the fish swirl at the surface, or if smaller fish are seen leaping from the water. Use this also where the fish are feeding in very shallow water (no more than three or four feet deep), or when fishing over thick beds of bladderwrack or kelp.

The second rod carries a fast sinking line: this will fish the fly close to the bottom and is essential in deep estuaries and bays with only slow tidal movements.

In estuaries with fast currents the fast sinking fly line comes into its own, for the flow will tend to make lighter density lines skate across the surface. Here you need a high density line to gain depth.

If (in fast flowing estuaries) you are letting the fly swing around on the flowing tide without retrieving (a), the fly will fish slightly deeper than if you are retrieving line with a slow figure-of-eight (b). And if fishing a water with no current, then a fly retrieved with a slow figure-of-eight will fish deeper than one retrieved quickly (c). Modify your choice of fly line according to the flow of the tide, and the depth and speed that you want the fly to fish.

Saltwater Flies

Flies that imitate natural foods can be used, including fish fry and shrimp patterns as well as lightly dressed lures that have been specially designed for sea trout such as the Medicine and Sunk Lures. It is worth tying salt water lures on stainless steel hooks.

Two easily tied lures that can be recommended are as follows:

Sea Trout Deceiver

Hook	Partridge "Sea Prince", sizes 1/0, 1, 2, 4 and 6
Thread	White
Tail	(tied at end of hookshank) 6-10 white saddle hackles with two grizzle hackles, one on each side, then three strands Lureflash Crystal Hair outside.

167

The sea trout Deceiver

Wing	A bunch of white hair tied all round the shank and extending beyond the bend with a small barred teal feather at the sides and 6-10 strands of peacock herl on top. Eyes may be painted on the teal feathers at the front.

A modification of Lefty Kreh's famous pattern, this is very effective for sea trout feeding on small fish, also for bass and mackerel.

Shrimp

Hook	Partridge "Sea Prince" sizes 2,4 and 6. Bend the hook shank with pliers as shown (middle). This kink, with the 'wing' tied on top, makes the lure fish point up and reduces snagging.
Thread	as body
Tail	bunch of bucktail as feelers. Incorporate two burned

Saltwater lures for sea trout. Top: shrimp types with bent 'keel' hook.
Below: Fry types

stubs of 30lb nylon as eyes.

Body   Lureflash Fritz

Wing   two or three pairs cock hackles

Tie this in a range of shrimpy colours: white hair and grizzle hackles with pearl Fritz; all pink; all brown; all olive.

Spinning and Bait Fishing

A 10ft rod with a test curve of 2 ½-3lb is the weapon to choose. It will be casting weights up to three ounces on 15lb to 25lb test line.

Spinners, Spoons and Plugs: Silver Mepps and Tobies are excellent. But note that sea feeding sea trout are very soft mouthed. Rapalas should always be carried, especially the 5 inch silver blue Husky Jerk and the 5½ inch needlefish or silver Sliver. The latter is, incidentally, designed for saltwater fishing (it has stainless steel hooks) and is the best plug for bass and sea trout fishing.

Baits: sand-eels and small fry (whitebait) can be bought from tackle shops in sea-side towns. Keep a supply in the deepfreeze.

Presentation

The fly and the spinner from the bank or when wading.

When fishing from the open shore it is tempting to cast straight out, simply because the fly or spinner lands furthest from land. Sometimes this is the best line of attack because the fish, lying in deeper water, will chase small fry from deep into shallow water. However sometimes the sea trout will swim close in, following the shore, and the 'straight out cast' may cover this line only for the last couple of yards of retrieve. Instead begin by casting at different angles so that on some retrieves the fly or spinner is brought back close in to the shore and on others it is brought from deep into shallower water.

a) The sea trout are chasing small fish from deep to shallow water. A long cast, 90° to the shore is more effective.

b) The sea trout are hunting the shallow water just offshore. The long cast at 90° to the shore is not as effective as a cast made 45° to the shore.

In saltwater fishing, the ability to cast a long line is a great asset on the grounds that the more water you cover the more fish will see the fly. But also important is the direction in which the cast is made: vary the casting angle to work out which is most effective on a particular day or in a particular location. And be prepared to move as you retrieve. Here MG casts a long line down-and-across the wind where the sea trout are moving up-wind in search of 'whitebait'. After letting the line sink he will retrieve and at the same time move slowly backwards ... now the fly will come back on a curve rather than straight route.

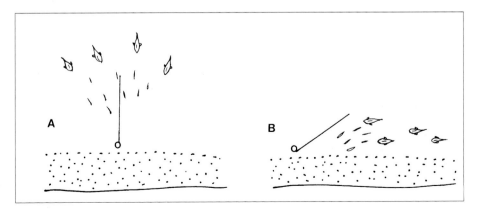

When fishing from the shore, unless you know that you are in a hot-spot such as the end of a promontory, keep on the move.

On most days, if you make a cast and retrieve without moving you will catch far less than if you cast and then move slowly, for a short distance (two or three yards), as you slowly retrieve the fly or spinner. How much less? In two trial days, moving fishing brought 37 sea trout whilst stationary fishing brought only three! And on another three days (five tides) moving fishing caught 22 bass and two sea trout whilst stationary fishing caught only seven bass!

It seems that sea trout (and bass) find a lure on a gradually changing track more attractive than one swimming on a straight track. In timed experiments the difference was quite marked: for one fish caught on a straight line retrieve, between four and 16 were caught on a curved retrieve (caused by the angler backing along the shore).

In (a) the angler stands at A and casts the fly or spinner to B. If he does not move whilst he retrieves, the fly or spinner will come back in a straight line AB.

In (b) the angler stands at A and casts the fly or spinner to B. Now he backs slowly along the beach whilst he retrieves and the fly or spinner will come back in an arc AB.

Even when fishing a hot-spot, where you are not moving along the shore, it is worth experimenting with changing the track of retrieve of the fly or spinner, rather than fishing just a straight line. There are two ways of achieving this.

Firstly, when fishing fairly slack water in bays or from beaches:

Cast out and begin the retrieve with the rod held out to one side of your body. But then, slowly swing the rod round to the other side of your body as you continue to retrieve. This will result in a slight change of track of the lure. Slight, but more attractive to the fish than a straight retrieve.

Secondly, in estuaries when the tide is flowing upstream on the flood and downstream on the ebb:

Fish this as a river. Face the direction of flow, so you will face up the estuary channel when the tide is flooding and down the channel when it is ebbing. Cast down-and-across the estuary channel. The current will then cause a belly to form in the line and the fly or spinner will swing around on the end of the line in an arc to the bank on which you are standing. As in rivers, the important point is to make sure that the fly or spinner swims across the flow in a balanced, controlled speed that mimics the little fish that the sea trout might be chasing. This is achieved by casting at a down-and-across angle that is appropriate to the flow rate.

The faster the current the more acute the angle of cast to keep the fly swimming across the channel on an even keel without it dragging out of control or, on a floating line, skating across the surface. And in the fastest of estuary channels (notably some with powerful tidal bores) it is sometimes necessary to make a long, down-and-across cast followed immediately by a large upstream mend in the line to slow the fly down.

Getting the speed of the fly and spinner right in estuaries is largely a matter of trial-and-error and experience. But in general it is perhaps true to say that, where the flow is slow most anglers fish too slowly and where the flow is fast most fish too quickly! The point about estuaries (compared with rivers above the tide) is that flow rates are constantly changing and direction of flow may change three times in one fishing session.

(a) The first stage of the flood: a fast current. The angler faces up the estuary and makes a long acute angled cast up the estuary channel.

(b) The latter stages of the flood : a slower current. The angler faces across the channel and makes an across or slightly up-and-across the estuary cast.

(c) The first stage of the ebb: a fast current. The angler faces down the estuary and makes a long acute angled cast down the estuary channel.

(d) The latter stages of the ebb: a slower current. The angler faces across the channel and makes an across or slightly down-and-across the estuary cast.

Presentation

The fly and the spinner from a boat

When fishing from an anchored boat it is easy to disregard casting direction and simply to cast the fly or spinner out at random. There are, however, three methods of presentation that are more effective than the random cast and retrieve.

1. Using the current: this is the method to use where the tide is flowing or there is a steady current.

The angler casts across the current to A, shooting an extra yard or two of slack line immediately the fly or spinner hits the water. The current will put a belly in the line and the fly or spinner will be pulled, or swing, around an arc AB on this belly. There is no need to retrieve in the early stages of this 'swing' in strong currents; in very slow currents, retrieve very slowly. But then, as the line begins to straighten at B retrieve more quickly and accelerate rapidly just before lift off to make the next cast. The bulk of offers will come as the fly or spinner swings around on the belly of line or, when sea trout are chasing the fly, in that final acceleration. Sometimes they will hit the lure just before it leaves the water prior to the next cast.

2. Using the wind when fishing the fly: this is the method to use where there is a strong breeze and little current.

The angler casts across the wind, aiming high so that the fly and leader fall downwind of the fly line (reduce power in the cast if you find that you are putting fly, leader and line in a straight line). The fly-line forms the line AB and the leader the arc BC. As the line lands on the water, an extra 1-2 yards of line are shot and thrown into a down-wind mend, converting the straight line AB into a curve AXB. The fly line and leader are now arranged in a sinuous path across the water. The fly and sinking line are allowed to sink before a slow retrieve is made. Instead of coming back on a straight line, the fly follows the sinuous path of the fly line (in practice the path of retrieve is not as sinuous as the original path of the line, especially when using a sinking fly line, but it is far from straight). About half way through the retrieve the speed of the fly is increased. Most offers will come as the

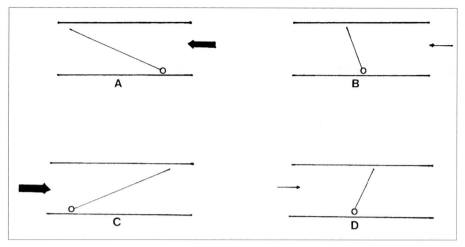

Casting angles on an estuary.

fly changes direction or, when fish are chasing the fly, in that final acceleration.

3. Round-the-clock fishing: this is the most effective method of fishing a small bay or estuary from an anchored boat in fairly calm conditions and fairly slack currents.

Imagine that the bow of the boat points to 12 o'clock and the stern to 6 o'clock. Cast and retrieve at 1 o'clock, 2 o'clock, 3 o'clock and so

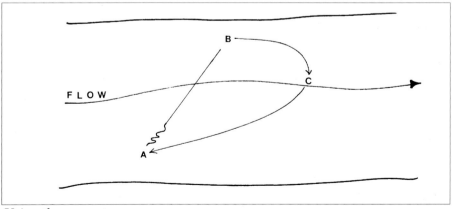

Using the current

on around the clock. This will cover the maximum amount of water from the boat, but also bring the fly or spinner back on a variety of paths.

Three important points when fishing fish imitations to sea trout:

1. Vary the rate of retrieve. On some days or some waters a slow retrieve takes the cake, and on others a fast retrieve.

2. Vary the line of retrieve: a constantly straight line is often the most ineffective.

3. If a fish follows the fly or spinner in without taking, accelerate the retrieve over the last few metres.

Boat fishing with bait for sea trout

Because sand-eels and fry are such an important food for sea trout, they are also an excellent bait, especially when fished from a boat.

Tackle consists of the spinning rod and reel loaded 15 lb BS line.

Method 1: The bouncing ledger.

A drilled bullet is fixed on the line with an SSG shot and a stainless steel bait hook .The hook is baited with a whole fresh sand-eel or whitebait. This rig is cast up-tide and allowed to bounce back along the bottom with the current. If the drilled bullet does not hit bottom at least once on each cast then put on a heavier one. When a fish takes there will be a heavy 'knock' and then a` pull. Strike immediately.

Method 2: The trailing sand-eel.

The rig is exactly the same as in Method 1, but the weight should be heavy enough to take the bait to midwater, but not the bottom. And instead of the single hook, a tandem mount is used consisting of a single hook in front (this is fixed through the lip of the bait) and a treble at the rear (fixed in the side of the bait). The bait is released down-tide and allowed to flutter in the current. Every few minutes another yard of line is released so that the bait fishes down over the flooded sand-banks where the sea trout are feeding. When a fish takes it usually does so with a wallop. The rod will pull round and set the hook.

A Rapala Silver can effectively be used instead of natural bait in Method 2.

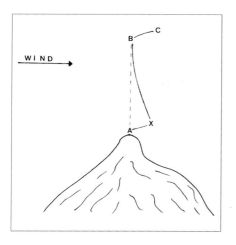

Using the wind

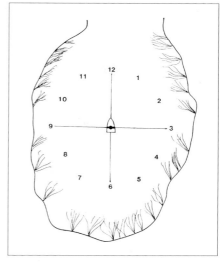

Round-the-clock fishing in a small weed-fringed bay.

Sea Trout Fishing in Salt Water

from *The Field,* November 1887

After a long drought how gratefully we receive the first shower. I had been passing some weeks in the Highlands near an arm of the sea, with sea trout lochs all around, which, owing to the dry weather, contained no fish. Burn-trout fishing, therefore, was all the sport to be obtained...Every day, when the tide was making, one could see salmon leaping in the sea loch, where large numbers of fish had collected, waiting for a rise of water in the river to commence the first stage of their journey to the spawning grounds. How we longed for a "saft" day. By an unusual piece of good luck wet weather set in before the end of my holiday, and I had some very fair sport in consequence. I well recollect how gleefully we saw the clouds gathering round the mountain tops one evening, and the soft feeling in the air, and the sweet smell rising from the refreshed heather, as a series of gentle showers fell on it the following morning. So far there was no increase in water in the rivers, and, instead of toiling up to a distant loch,as we had intended, we decided to devote a morning to spinning in the sea loch...

As the gillie rowed us slowly from the shore, my friend put up a small phantom minnow, while I experimentally fastened a 'Halcyon' to the end of a light spinning trace, sand eels, the best bait of all, not being obtainable. Tackle fixed, I took one oar, laid the rod between my knees, and with the gillie, pulled the boat across the mouth of the river where the salmon were leaping wildly, dancing with delight, perhaps, at the prospect of the approaching change to fresh water. With regard to the salmon, I may say at once that we caught none, but were more fortunate with the sea trout...Though we took no salmon, our endeavours to attract that most lordly of fish led to our discovering that the sea trout is by no means particular in his choice of baits. I had put up a Halcyon spinner, a bunch of peacock herl combined with red and yellow feathers, which, having two fans at its head, spins brilliantly ...We had not made one turn across the mouth of the river before a small sea trout took my lure, but, after a leap or two, went off ... After pricking another fish I changed my bait for a small Devon minnow of unusual attractiveness, being covered as to its back with transparent golden-brown paint, through which shone the silver of the metal. My first fish was a cuddy, or youthful coalfish. Finding that the salmon would not look at our baits near the mouth of the river, we rowed lower down the sea loch to a spot where we had seen a salmon or two leaping. On the way two more sea trout were assisted into the boat by means of the landing net, my friend's phantom and my little golden-brown Devon. The salmon on our new fishing ground were no more amenable to reason than those at the mouth of the river. After giving the Devon and small phantom a trial, I put up a large red phantom while my friend tried a large gold and silver clipper bait. To our surprise, both baits were taken by sea trout. Later, I exchanged the red phantom for the small cuddy I had taken earlier in the day, rigged up on a Chapman spinner ... Neither salmon nor pollack took it, but a sea trout of about three quarters of a pound did, which somewhat astonished me, as the tackle was particularly coarse, and the bait considerably larger than I generally use for jack. I need not further follow the events of that morning's fishing. We fished for salmon, and, as a result, had twelve sea trout, averaging about one pound each, caught on the Halcyon bait, Devon baits, large red phantom, small brown phantom, Clipper, and a small coalfish. But, after all, is not the charm of angling its uncertainty?"

John Bickerdyke

Postscript: The sports of river, lake and saltwater sea trout fishing depend on clean rivers generating the sea trout smolts that go to sea, and the sea providing sufficient food to generate the returning run of adult sea trout to river and lake.

Until fairly recently, few but anglers cared about the cleanliness of freshwaters. It was by mere chance and the (often unheeded) protestations of anglers that sea trout (and salmon) have survived in many rivers. Today 'green' environmental matters are to the fore, despite the fact that politicians generally make only appeasing noises and are slow to act. Yet through the efforts of bodies such as the Anglers' Conservation Association (ACA) and Salmon & Trout Association the devastations of the past are being corrected, and more rivers producing more and more smolts.

At sea it is a different matter. Salmon farms, through their use of toxic chemicals and infestations of sea lice, have wiped out the sea trout stocks of much of western Scotland and the Northern Isles, and greatly reduced the sea trout populations off parts of western Ireland. And fishing fleets from the European Union (most notably from the so-called 'green' country of Denmark) are hoovering up increasing tonnages of sand-eels and other lesser fish on which sea trout, bass, other sea fish and a host of sea birds rely. The weak-minded national and EU governments are failing in their responsibility of controlling such environmental damage.

We anglers are slowly winning the battle for clean rivers and lakes. Now the battle is for the seas. And it is our responsibility to take part in this battle by lobbying our national and European Members of Parliament. We owe it to the fish.

PART THREE

FISHING WITH FALKUS

been played when there may be some slack coils down near the back-ing. A turn of line pulled hard into loose coils underneath will cause the reel to jam while a fish is running, resulting almost invariably in a smash. It's cost a lot of big fish.

For Spring and late Autumn fishing, with a sinking line, only a short leader is necessary. Five or six feet of, say, 20lb breaking strain monofil is ample. For summer fishing with floating line and small flies, it is advisable to have nine or 10 feet of leader, the thickness depending on the size of fly. A small fly won't swim attractively on heavy nylon, so when we go down in size of fly, we go down in nylon thickness.

Having tied on a fly and placed the hook in the little ring usually provided just above the rod butt, wind the reel tight. Now, unless you are going to start fishing at once, twist a pipe cleaner around the rod and leader just above the fly. This will prevent the fly from coming loose and catching in the bushes or your clothing or your ear as you walk along; very painful, and it wastes time.

But what fly do we choose, and how do we choose it? In an attempt to answer this question, a vast amount of mumbo-jumbo has been amassed. Few writers are as frank as Kelson who wrote:

"It is impossible to lay down any hard and fast rule for selecting a fly. The best of us are often at our wits' end to know what fly to select."

And, quite frankly, so are most of us. All the same, we must have confidence in our fly because if we don't, we won't fish it hard enough. But what confidence can anyone have in a fly that hasn't been chosen for some particular reason, be it fact or fancy? but what rea-son? Size? Shape? Colour? Certain colours are sometimes recom-mended on the grounds that they enable a fish to see the fly better and that brightly coloured flies will therefore result in more offers. In my opinion, this is very doubtful. Salmon have excellent vision. They may refuse a fly for any number of reasons, but an inability to see it well enough is not likely to be among them. I have caught fish with a number eight fly on a floating line in water the colour of cocoa, when other anglers were spinning. Again, salmon are undoubtedly colour-conscious, but does anyone know what colour - if any - is likely to stimulate them at any given moment? Some pundits advocate a bright fly for a bright day and a dull fly for a dull day, whereas others prefer a dull fly on a bright day and a bright fly on a dull day. Does it really make any difference? The angler who cocks a snook at colour and relies on a plain Stoat's Tail all the summer seems to catch his share of fish.

It is probable that if we select any one well-tried pattern of fly and fish it in varying sizes and degrees of dressing throughout the season we will do just as well as we would if we had a host of patterns to choose from. Indeed, we're likely to do better since we shall not waste so much time wondering which pattern to choose or whether what we have on at any particular time is really giving us the best chance of hooking a fish. But most people like to see a touch of colour in a fly, if only to give themselves more heart - and so do I. I am but human, and like all other salmon fishermen I've known I have cases crammed with flies of every sort.

In early Spring I mostly fish tandem lures or tube flies of two to four inches in length with slender black bodies ribbed with silver or gold topped by long hair wings of black, yellow and orange. I feel sure that some, if not all, of these colours are unnecessary, but the result looks attractive - at least it does to me, and since it's a very simple pattern and easy to tie - and successful - I seldom use anything else. For the small fly fished on the floating line in late Spring and Summer I am content with something like a Hairy Mary or a Munro Killer or a Stoat's Tail, dressed on double hooks in sizes four to 12 or roughly one and half inches down to about half an inch. Again, I feel certain I don't really need all these patterns, but they please me and they please the salmon - although I don't believe the salmon care tuppence abut pattern. What I think matters about a fly on any particular day is its size, its amount of dressing and the way it is fished. Of course, what also matters is where and when it is fished, which is entirely another matter. Some people claim a knowledge of salmon-taking times that, to my mind, borders on the supernatural. I don't believe there is anyone alive who can predict when salmon will and will not take. If you fish day after day the season through on various rivers as I have done, you will find that according to the time of year, certain periods of the day tend to offer better chances than others due, perhaps, to changes in light and temperature, or to a rise of water caused by melting snow high up in the hills, and so on. But does this mean that we fish only at these times? Of course not. A salmon may take at any time of the day and occasionally - as I shall discuss when dealing with sea trout fishing - at night as well. At best these so-called "taking times" are only a very rough guide.

On a cold and miserable morning not long ago, I had two fish on the bank before breakfast. Afterwards, when the day had, as I thought, improved, I fished until dark without an offer. The following day on the same water, I fished from daybreak and took my only salmon with the last cast of the evening. We never know for certain when the magic moment will come. Always provided there's a run of fish, what catches salmon is water sense, presentation and sheer persistence. And, of course, confidence - without which persistence dwindles. After we have fished for hours without an offer it is natural to wonder whether failure is due to the fly or the salmon or - heaven forfend - perhaps even us. In spite of the inherent reluctance of salmon to take a fly, failure to catch them is frequently our own fault; walking along a high bank against the skyline; clumsy wading; rattling on the bottom with an iron-shod wading stick; unnecessary false casting so that the line flashes to and fro just above the lies - sometimes even thrashing the water as it does so; fishing with a bright sun behind the rod so that flickering shadows precede us down the pool. All these may frighten salmon, and we cannot catch frightened fish.

We shall improve our chances if we behave like hunters and acquire stealth. When the novice starts to think and act like a good hunter, he needn't worry whether he'll make a good fisherman - he'll be well on the way to being one. But however stealthy we may be and whatever fly we choose, we still have to present that fly to a salmon and since no-one knows for certain where or when a taking salmon is going to be found, the fly should be made to work attractively all the time it is fishing. It must travel at a controlled speed and depth across every place a salmon may be lying and it is precisely because the expert salmon fisherman can do this - through his water sense and casting skill - that he catches so many salmon. His success is often ascribed to luck by the less accomplished angler but as I have already implied, there is more than mere luck in successful salmon fishing. Of course, in a wide pool - unless we are fishing from a boat - it is impossible to cover every lie, so that our chances of success (that is the number of fish our fly covers attractively) will depend upon our effective casting range. Needless to say, the ability to cast a long and accurate line is of great value but 'effective' casting range is not the overall distance cast, however far that may be, it is an imaginary line drawn down the river parallel with our own bank inside which our fly is working at the right speed and depth; in other words, in a manner likely to attract a fish. Merely to cast across a strong current and leave the fly to swing round is of little use. As soon as the line touches down the current starts to drag it round in a huge bow and the fly follows at excessive speed, often coming up and skidding across the surface when we're using a floating line and swimming far too close to the top when we're using a sinker - and in neither case are we likely to hook a salmon. We may have cast a distance of, say, 30 yards across the river, but almost all this distance has been wasted because the fly was not working attractively until it was almost straight down stream from the rod. Measured across the river, our effective casting range was nothing like 30 yards; it was perhaps no more than eight. So, any salmon lying more than eight yards out are not going to be caught by us. Our fly may pass over them, but they will never take it. We can increase our effective casting range in two ways: first of all by mending the line.

Mending is done with a circular movement of the rod immediately a cast has been completed. The belly formed by the current is switched over so that the downstream curve becomes an upstream curve. This has the effect of slowing down the fly and allowing it to swing across the river at an acceptable speed and depth. In a strong draw, several more upstream mends may be necessary as the fly comes round, but this can only be down with a floating line; with a quick sinking line more than one mend is seldom possible. When fishing heavy water I find it helpful to keep two or three yards of line trapped against the rod under my forefinger as I cast. As soon as the line touches down, I make an upstream mend, shooting this slack line as I do so. This dodge is very useful for helping to put an upstream curve into a quick sinking line. Some people find it difficult to mend a quick sinking line when they are Spey casting. This is because they tend to roll the line out along the surface so that by the time the line has straightened out, part of it has sunk. This is not the best way of completing a Spey cast. As the forward stroke is made, the line should be aimed slightly upwards so that it straightens out in the air. The result is precisely the same as the finish of the overhead cast. Of course, if there's only a moderate current, no mending is necessary. The fly will fish perfectly well if we cast it out at whatever angle is best for that amount of water, leave it alone and let the stream swing it out. But, irrespective of the current, and whether or not we need to mend the line, we shall increase our range if we wade into the river. Once we have mastered the knack of controlling our fly, it follows that provided we don't disturb the fish, the deeper we wade, the more water our fly can cover effectively.

From January until about mid April, a quick sinking line will be the order of the day and during this often bitterly cold period of ice and snow, we shall use big flies ranging in size from four inches down to two inches in length, mainly on tubes. Broadly speaking, the size of fly is determined by the water temperature. Salmon will not rise or rush about very much in cold water, so if it is to be taken, our fly must be offered to them at a convenient depth and speed. When we are fishing one of the big salmon rivers from a boat in early Spring - especially when the water is very low and the fish concentrated in the deepest part of a pool - it often pays to anchor the boat upstream of the lie and fish cast after cast very slowly. Give the line plenty of time to sink and then strip it in from the dangle an inch or two at a time. A salmon may not take until several yards have been stripped in and not by any means the first time over. So keep at it - this is one of the few occasions when it is profitable to concentrate on one particular spot. After a while the inch-by-inch technique seems to tantalize a fish and goad it into taking.

As the the world spins and air and water temperatures rise, salmon start to move about more freely. Our fly is still fished on sunk line but needs to be neither as large nor sunk as deep as hitherto. And then, sometime between April and May, when the water temperature is in the middle 40s, salmon will start to take a much smaller fly, fished close to the surface, and henceforth, until late Autumn, most of our fishing will be done with small flies from size four to 12 presented on a floating line at a depth of about four inches.

Fishing the floating line is much easier than fishing the sunk line - so much so that many anglers, delighting in the use of their rods, become fascinated by casting and stay for too long in one place. Taking too long over fishing a pool is a common fault. It is far better to fish down a piece of water twice quickly than once very slowly. By this I don't mean that the fly should be fished quickly, I mean that the angler should keep on the move, taking two or three paces between each cast and not covering the same place time after time as so many novices do. Of course, there are exceptions to this and one occurs when a salmon rises to the fly but refuses it. Obviously that fish is a potential taker, so what should we do about it?

Well, there's no hard and fast rule. What I usually do is move backwards a few yards and then fish down to the lie again with the same fly but this time getting the fly to work in a different way. To do this, I cast more squarely across the current, make a big mend and then another - shooting extra line each time to encourage the fly to sink - then, as the fly comes round towards the lie, I strip in a yard or two of line so that as it covers the fish, the fly is swimming up towards the surface. This little ploy will sometimes induce the fish to take. If there is no reaction, I retreat again and change to a smaller fly. If this is refused, I try a larger fly. If this too fails, I carry on down the pool. How long we continue to cast to such a fish depends on circumstances. If there isn't much doing and offers are very rare, I'll give some time to it, but if there are plenty of fish about and the chances are good, I give this one a couple of casts and leave it - it can always be tried again later.

I should make it clear that I don't stop casting to a fish because I am concerned about over-fishing the lie. I don't believe it's possible to over-fish a salmon lie - or a sea trout lie for that matter, provided the lie is covered properly - that is, the fish is not frightened.

More than once in clear water when salmon have been visible I have cast time after time over a fish I thought might be a taker- and succeeded in catching it. On one well remembered occasion my wife Kathleen watched me cast continuously for a 20 -pounder. She had the fish under observation all the time until, after about 50 minutes, it took. So, if a fish rises but refuses there is a very real chance that he may come again and take the fly if he is still there and hasn't been frightened. And if he does, it's one of the most exciting moments that any sportsman can ever experience. The take of a salmon is as gentle as a kiss and if we want to hook the fish, there's one golden rule entirely without exception: we must never strike.

I keep a loop of line tucked under my finger to prevent a snatch if a salmon takes. Like a little shaft of light, the fly flickers slowly across the pool a few inches below the surface, and when a salmon takes, there is just a tiny pluck and the loop of line slides out. You can't believe it's a salmon, it's so gentle. Then you lift the rod and the line is solid and you think you've hooked a rock, and then rock moves away and you realize you're into a salmon, and it's pure magic.

When playing a salmon - or, for that matter, any other fish - we should never let him see us. Sometimes a fish allows himself to be brought close into the bank very early on. This apparent submission is quite usual and may be described as the danger time. At this moment, far from lunging at him with net or gaff, we should keep well back and do nothing. As soon as he feels the water shallowing underneath him, he'll be off again on a long run across the river - and we must let him go. The more he rushes about like this the better; the sooner he will tire. We have plenty backing on the reel and have complete confidence in our tackle for we checked everything before we started. Again we bring the fish towards us, trying to keep him on the move, not letting him stay still so that he can rest and recover his strength.

It's a good plan to 'walk' a fish whenever possible. It seems to take the heart out of him and shortens the fight. It also enables us to to do battle in water of our choosing. When we walk a fish we hold the rod steady and at right angles to the river with the butt set firmly against the body. the fish is not towed up the pool; we're not indulging in a trial of strength, but the art of gentle persuasion. So long as a steady but unhurried progress is maintained upstream, our fish will usually follow quietly. but, of course, it doesn't always work. I once hooked a 30-pounder on very light tackle. I couldn't do anything with him. He got down beside a rock in very fast water and wouldn't budge. Eventually, to shift him and try and keep him moving, I swam the pool six times fully clothed and taking my rod with me. This was in March in snow and it nearly killed me, but I landed the fish. However, it's not a method I'd recommend. Nor should such a desperate method be needed. After all, it was my own fault - I should have been using tackle of sensible breaking strain.

When the salmon starts to half roll in the current and we see the flash of a silver flank, he is nearly ready to land. Nearly, but not quite. This is the crucial time. Don't try to haul him in too soon. When he feels the stones under his belly he'll flap violently and may throw the hook. Wait until he turns on his side. Whenever there's a place convenient for beaching the salmon, no landing tackle of any sort is necessary unless it is a very large fish. We draw him ashore at the place we've chosen and when he's lying on his side, with his head aground, the fight is over - he'll not move again.

To close matters, we approach, reeling in as we go, then - keeping sufficient line out by holding the rod at arm's length inshore we take the wrist of the tail firmly with thumb and forefinger - the back of the

HF with angling companions at Cragg. Left, with Fred. J. Taylor in winter.
Right, with Fred Buller (left) and Richard Walker, early 1970's.

hand uppermost - push the fish forward up the shore clear of the water, then pick him up. It is a very simple operation.

Now, a tap on the head from the priest and there, fresh from the sea with the tide lice still on his flanks, is the fish we spend so much time and thought and money trying to catch.

Salmo the Leaper - the Atlantic salmon. Of all fishes, one of the most mysterious and elusive. Certainly the most aggravating.

Five in a Bed

A sense of the ridiculous is not essential to successful salmon fishing but it helps. For one thing, it conditions the mind when we are think-ing of salmon and how to catch them. What is surprising about this sport is not that we catch so few salmon, but that we ever catch any at all. After all, offering something resembling food to a non-feeding fish borders on lunacy. Nevertheless, there are times when, for reasons unknown, salmon are absurdly easy to hook.

I am not suggesting that they return from the sea with their brains addled. But there is no doubt that from our point of view as anglers, when salmon regain fresh water their behaviour becomes ridiculous. As A. H. Chaytor wrote in *Letters to a Salmon Fisher's Sons*: 'One thing you may be sure of about a salmon, you can never tell either what he will do, or when he will do it.'

For me, this sense of never being quite sure what is going to happen plays a major part in the charm and excitement of salmon fishing. If this sense is ever stripped away, though the mystery of the salmon may remain, the magic of its capture will dissolve. A strange, not to say unique, experience of this happened to me not long ago on a well known border river.

I was one of four rods fishing a private beat for the day. The other three rods, cheery Lancashire lads I'd not met before, were fishing as a party. I was alone. What with one thing and another I didn't turn up on the river until about six o'clock, just as they were heading for their 'tea' in the local.

'Hullo!' they chorused as I got out of the car. 'Look who's here !'
'Any luck?' I enquired.
'No,' they said, 'It's hopeless. We've fished every inch of it. You'll catch nowt.'
'Water looks perfect to me,' I ventured.
'Oh aye,' they agreed. 'It is. But there's nowt in it. We started before breakfast. Flogged all day. Haven't had a touch. Coming back later for a go at the sea trout. If there are any!'
'May see you later then.'
'Good luck,' they shouted, climbing into their Range Rover. 'Hey Hey! You'll need it!'

They drove away roaring with laughter. The thought of Falkus flogging a stretch of empty water while they were boozing happily in the pub seemed to have made their day. Thoughtfully, I set up some tackle and turned my attention to the river.

Making my way upstream I passed a couple of long, deep pools. These I felt sure had been well hammered. Then came some faster, broken water, ideal for grilse and sea trout, a fine place to fish on an August evening but not what I was looking for just then. I came to a long rather shallow glide where between steep, high banks dense with trees, the water flowed steady and unbroken over a bed of firm gravel.

At a gap in the trees I stopped and stood looking at this stretch or what I could see of it: a comparatively narrow strip of open water hemmed in by leafy branches which hung out from either bank. About 20 yards downstream of the gap, a short run of water under the trees on the far bank attracted my attention. This possible 'taking strip', only eight or 10 yards in length, had a faintly darker, more swirly look about it, as though at that point the river flowed over a slight depression, perhaps a shallow rocky tough, a perfect resting lie for running fish. The longer I gazed at it, trying to picture the river bottom at that place, the more promising it looked.

Grilse are a law unto themselves but the fish I was hoping, indeed expecting, to catch were big, fresh run autumn salmon. Such fish, it seemed to me, would have run through the hurly-burly of the faster water downstream and, since they were not lying in the deep pools below - the Lancashire lad's experience seemed proof of that - could well have finished up in the comfortable measured flow under those tree branches on the other bank. It looked right. If I were a running salmon, I thought to myself, that is where I would choose to rest.

I wondered whether the lads, when fishing every inch of the beat, had included the glide. I thought it unlikely. And some elementary detective work on the bankside vegetation at the gap - the only spot where it was possible to slide into the river- confirmed this view. The grass was uncrushed, there were no scuffles, no footprints. My pulse, as they say, quickened. Instinctively, I began to feel that I was in with a chance.

Already my mind had been working like a computer. Should I hook a fish in those difficult conditions I knew exactly how I would play and land it. I slid into the water, which was thigh deep against the bank, removed the lanyard from my landing net, stuck the net handle into the bankside and then tied one end of the lanyard to a tree root, leaving the other end trailing in the water. After that I waded out waist deep to the end of the tree branches and made my way carefully down stream.

On the other bank, under the trees, not far above my assumed taking strip, lodged among the tree roots by some recent spate was a white plastic fertilizer bag. Usually I view such unsightly objects with regret but in this case I welcomed it. It made an excellent casting marker; a point to aim at.

The water in that short taking strip where I thought the fish were lying was, I reckoned, between five and six feet deep,.I wanted my fly to fish about two feet off the bottom. That, to me, is the ideal presentation for sunk-line fishing in cold water.

Yes, I know salmon in these conditions will sometimes come up and take a fly on or just under the surface. I've caught them there. Sometimes, but most of the time, for my money, the fly fishes deep. I'm not talking about 'scraping the bottom', that's nonsense. A few inches above the fishes' noses is where I wanted the fly to pass. And to me, a fly that is fishing four feet down in six feet of water is deep.

When I was within casting range of the white marker I stripped off sufficient line and let it it drift with the fly straight downstream, sinking as it went. Then, with both wrists, I rolled it to the surface, whisked it back upstream into a figure of eight loop and with a tilted rod, Spey cast it towards the opposite bank.

I call this cast the 'square cut', that beautiful and deeply satisfying stroke wide of point, remembered from my cricketing days. The sight of the line snaking out a foot or so above the water, then curling in under the branches so that the fly popped down close to the white bag filled me with delight.

There was an interval of breathless anticipation, lasting perhaps five or six seconds as the fly sank and swung round under the branches. Then suddenly - wow!

As usual when a salmon takes there was nothing dramatic. With a tightening of the line the fly just stopped as though caught in the bottom. I raised the rod - and there he was! A big fellow, lugging away on the line almost as though in slow motion.

What was so wonderful about that particular take was the realisation that my water sense had won an Oscar. But of course, as always when a salmon takes my fly, I experienced the three intense emotions of disbelief, magic and jubilation, fused into a single moment of triumph.

But in the present situation there was no time to dwell on self-praise. If a fish of that size ran downstream there was no chance of following him. I had to walk him upstream, as I had planned to do, and land him at the gap. Immediately I turned sideways-on to the current and with my rod held at right angles to the river, waded steadily back upstream to the gap in the trees.

The fish followed faithfully, like a dog. (A walked fish will nearly always come with you if taken in hand soon enough). But when I reached the gap I stopped. And the fish, as I expected, suddenly woke up. This was the place where I had already decided to fight and land the fish. There was no question of letting him run far. He had to be landed on the spot. I was, of course, using immensely strong tackle.

As always, every item had been tested before I started fishing. The fly line stripped off the reel and re-wound evenly and firmly, the leader was a yard or so of new sea-fishing nylon that would have held a shark. The treble hook in the two-inch plain black and orange tube could have held a bucket full of coal. There was plenty of backing. All knots had been carefully tied and from experience were the best I knew. In my philosophy there are many reasons but very few excuses for being broken - the angler's ultimate disgrace. Usually it is due to lack of attention to detail. Well, nobody could accuse me of that.

Apart from avoiding being broken, I use such strong tackle to reduce playing time to a minimum. Therefore, if I choose to release a fish, I can do so without its having suffered unduly.

The fish I'd hooked was upwards of 20lbs, I reckoned, but I gave not an inch of ground. He rushed off across the river like a torpedo and ran upstream under the trees. This was just what I wanted. He slowed down and stopped after about 30 yards, whereupon I lowered the rod and holding it sideways to the fish, put a finger on the reel and pulled. A few seconds of this leverage turned the fish so that he swung round and, still heading obliquely upstream, charged across to my own bank. Now, from my point of view, he was in the best possible position. I quickly wound up the slack line I had stripped in when he'd come across, and applied maximum pressure. The longer you take (and most people take far too long) the more time he has to shed the hook. If I gave this fish too much stick and the hook pulled through its hold, well let it. Whatever happened, pusillanimity was not going to be responsible for losing him.

Relying on the strength of my terminal tackle, I kept pulling his head downstream. The net handle was gripped between my legs and as the fish swung out from underneath the branches I ignored the plunging and kicking and dragged him straight back across the rim. I raised the net - and there he was, a great big cock fish folded up inside and splashing madly, but mine!

I stuffed the rod butt down inside my breast waders and killed the fish with the priest hanging around my neck. This was the most difficult part of the proceedings, achieved by jamming the net's rim against the bank and so, with the handle clamped between my thighs, giving myself the use of both hands. From start to finish the fish had taken only a few minutes to land simply because, never having seen me, he had remained unscared. Puzzled maybe, but not frightened, the most important aspect of any quick landing. Invisible against the loom of the bank, I had kept out of sight the whole time.

After that it was easy, I removed the hook and threaded the loose end of the net cord - which I had previously tied to the tree root through the fish's gills. Then, letting the dead fish wave gently in the current, I tied the cord back on the root alongside the original knot.

Fifty minutes later I was standing in the same place, but now there were five big salmon trailing side by side on the net lanyard in the streamy water below that tree root. Four more casts I had made towards the plastic bag, and each cast had rung up the three roses.

At last the scales had fallen from my eyes. Clearly this was one of those rare occasions when I had managed to sneak in and catch fate off her guard. Usually, as most salmon fishers know to their cost, one arrives on location only to be told that conditions were very good yesterday and will probably be even better tomorrow, but, 'Hidden by God', are no good today. Well, for me, today was perfect for that lie under the branches. Almost certainly it was only a very temporary resting place, whose tenancy depended on an exact height (and probably temperature) of water. A shoal of big fish lying there today, no fish lying there tomorrow. Almost certainly they would have run upstream later that evening.

Quite possibly there hadn't been a single fish lying there all season, and there might not be another before the season's end. For once, old Falkus had hit the jackpot.

By now the setting sun was a dull blush in the clouds and most of the river had dissolved into shadow. Quite suddenly, it seemed, the current gurgling underneath the far branches had become black and mysterious. Between the tree-lined banks I had the sensation of wading in a tunnel, casting across jig-saw patches of light and shade into a distant crevice of darkness.

For the sixth time, aimed at the white plastic bag, my fly curled under the branches, sank and swung round. And for the sixth time, in the same place as before, dead on cue - it stopped!

For the sixth time I went through the, by now familiar routine but, as I walked the gently lugging fish upstream towards the gap, I realised that there was no longer the excitement. It was all too easy. It had indeed become, simply, a routine.

This time, as I drew the tiring fish in towards the net I could see that it wasn't well hooked. A big hen fish, it turned broadside on and hung there in the current just short of the net. The hook was plainly visible, fastened only by a sliver of skin. The fish was tantalizingly close, but for me to pull harder could only court disaster. To allow the fish more freedom seemed equally futile. A second or two later, however, our impasse was ended as the wisp of skin broke free. For a moment or two the fish dropped back sideways with the stream, then with a flick of its tail it swung round in a flash of silver and was gone.

To lose a big fish is always a wrench, but I honestly didn't regret the loss of that fish. It was the one female I'd hooked, and even in the moment of frustration I'd known I would have freed her unharmed.

Conscious that I was going to miss the best hour of the day, I cut off the fly, put it away and wound in the line. I didn't want to wade down that strip of water again. I knew that if I put out another cast towards that plastic bag I should hook another fish. I knew, and suddenly I didn't want to do it. I had hooked six fish in six casts, landing five averaging more than 20 pounds. What more was there left to prove? There would be smoked salmon for all my friends at Christmas. I'd caught enough. Losing that fish had sealed the issue. It was time to stop.

Of course had the spirit moved me, I could have gone on and played at catch-and-release. But to do that purposely is to change angling from a sport into a game, and that is something I could never do.

I pitched the landing net up on top of the bank, threw the wading staff after it, and then the rod. With the river curling round my thighs I stood where I was for a little while, thinking about it all.

Quite apart from the size of the fish it had been a strange experience, almost uncanny. But there was no witchcraft wound up in the way those fish were caught. Success had hung on two things: water sense and good casting. I looked across the darkening river to the white plastic bag that glimmered faintly in the dusk. Anyone who could have Spey cast a sinking line and put the fly under those tree branches would have done just as well as I had. It was an example of why casting ability is sometimes the key factor in hooking salmon. If I hadn't been able to make that particular type of Spey cast, I'd have caught nothing. It was as simple as that.

I crawled up the bank and, with great difficulty, hauled the fish up after me. Then, looking like the Ancient Mariner with his albatross, I slung them round my neck and lugged them back to the car. By the time I got there I must have felt worse than he did. Even an albatross doesn't weigh a hundredweight!

No sooner had I got the fish packed into the boot, and settled myself thankfully into the driving seat, when back from the pub came the wedding ... sorry, the fishing guests.

'Ah, there he is!' they chorused. 'The man himself! Look! He's packing up!' They disentangled themselves from their seat belts and staggered across.

'Had enough of it, then?'

'Yes,' I said, 'I've had enough'

'We told you so,' they crowed. 'Ha Ha! We told you there was nowt in the river.'

'You did,' I agreed, starting the car. 'You certainly did. All the same, if I were you I'd try that reach upstream between the trees before it gets too dark. It looks promising.'

'No,' they demurred. 'It's all grown up, you can't fish it. Anyway it wouldn't be worthwhile, there's nothing come in.'

'Never you mind,' said one of them consolingly. 'Even you can't catch what isn't there'.

'That's very true,' I said. 'Well good luck, lads.'

I let in the clutch and drove away into the darkening leaving them there chortling with glee at the thought of the big-headed old bugger getting his come-uppance.

Later that night the fishery manager rang me to find out how I'd got on. I told him. 'Good God!' he said. 'I heard you'd packed up early and caught nothing. What happened, did the fish just stop taking?'

'No. I stopped fishing.'

'You stopped!' he exclaimed incredulously. 'In the middle of it all? You don't expect me to believe that, do you?'

'No,' I said 'I suppose I don't really. But that's what happened.'

There was a silence. Then, 'Hey, listen,' he burst out. 'The other rods told me that they fished all day long. They're experienced anglers. Nobody had a touch. You're having me on.'

I put him right about that, and finally convinced him I really had caught some fish, but pointed out that the whole thing had simply got out of hand. For once, quite by chance, nature had been turned upside down. There was no longer any challenge. I'd had a fish with every cast and the magic had gone.

I went on like this for some time, trying to explain why, at the peak of success - during a season when so little had been caught - I'd stopped fishing. But he still didn't seem to understand.

CHAPTER 14

SEA TROUT FISHING WITH FALKUS

HF's beloved river Esk, Cumbria.

A Night on the River

I arrive on the river bank at dusk in the hush of late evening with the sun sinking behind the fells and the valley in shadow. "Parting day," Thomas Gray wrote, "leaves the world to darkness and to me." But of course it doesn't. Evening brings its own solitude, but you're never really alone on a river. Although mostly unseen, out come the creatures of darkness that keep us company at the waterside. An owl hoots from shadowy woods; no other sound except the murmur of the river

- and then suddenly, the splash of a sea trout in the pool below. That could be a running fish; on the other hand it could be lying there restless and perhaps ready to take. Well, I shall find out ...

To start fishing too soon in that low, clear water is a great mistake, but it's dark enough now. I fish with tense anticipation, at each cast expecting that sea trout to take the fly. I can no longer see the pitch of the line, but I can feel the movement of the fly as it swings across the pool.

To fish well at night demands absolute concentration. Even the cry of an owl can be distracting, but there's nothing quite as disrupting as the sound of a human voice, which is why my two labradors are the ideal companions - they don't chatter. Suddenly a fish moves just above me - a good one by the sound of it. Now that could be a taking fish!

To stalk a fish in a known lie is so tremendously exciting ... I'm getting near to him now; the next cast should cover him. There ... I want the fly to flicker temptingly past his nose. Now, surely ... Yes! I've got

The old fishing caravan on the knoll above Donald's pool (now demolished)

him! He's a good fish alright. Sea trout fight like tigers - it's so easy
to lose them when they leap - but he's nearly ready to land, if he'll
only stay on while I get the net under him ... Now's the time when they
come off, just as you draw them into the shallows - but not this one.
Its silver flank flashes in the moonlight - a perfect sea trout between
six and seven pounds, straight from some distant tide rip. Of all fish
and fishing, this - for me - is the very top: the enchantment of sea trout
night fly-fishing.

Although sea trout can be caught in daylight in a number of different ways, to me, of all methods, the fly at night is the most skillful and
the most exciting. The lures I fish for sea trout at night and the ways
in which I fish them are those I have used over the last 40- odd years.
But before considering these ways and means, let's take a glance at the
fish itself.

The sea trout is a migratory brown trout, but there its likeness to a
brown trout ends. It is similar in appearance to the salmon, but has
very different habits, and it is important for the novice to understand
that sea trout fly-fishing is neither a branch of brown trout nor of
salmon fishing. It is a sport entirely of its own.

While in fresh water waiting to spawn, sea trout eat very little - for
the very good reason that there is very little for them to eat. Many sea
trout rivers are clear, rocky, acid, barren spate rivers that hold only a
tiny proportion of the food necessary to support a sea trout population
with normal appetites. Apart from the younger fish - herling, whitling,
finnock or what have you, many of which continue to feed in fresh
water as avidly as the food supply permits - the majority of sea trout
on their return from sea live on the store of nourishment accumulated
in their tissues. Of course, not all waters present the same picture. The
behaviour of many species of animals depends partly on their environment and the sea trout is no exception. In some of the food-rich
river and lake systems of north west Britain, sea trout take more interest in food than sea trout found in most of our spate rivers, but I suggest that the reason for this interest in a food item or, for that matter,
an angler's lure, is similar to that well-known mountaineer's interest

in his mountain: "Because it is there." If it's not there the returning sea trout make little or no effort to search for it and this is the dfference between the behaviour of sea trout and brown trout.

The difference between sea trout and salmon is that whereas the salmon tends to take a lure mainly by day the sea trout, with certain exceptions, does so mainly by night. Thus, a sound basis from which to think about how to catch sea trout is the concept of a non-feeding fish which takes a lure from habit rather than hunger and is active in the darkness; and I have learnt from experience that although not every night offers the same opportunities, there are few nights when sea trout cannot be caught - always provided the fish are present and the river is not in flood. No other conditions absolutely preclude the catching of sea trout at night and, although it would be foolish to pretend that some weather conditions are not more unpropitious than others, we should never allow them to deter us from fishing. They will reduce our chances, certainly, but if we are skillful enough, we can still catch fish. And talking about weather, it's worth noting that although fly-fishing is usually poor during periods of heavy rain, it can be very good when the rain stops. Sea trout often take well just after a thunderstorm has passed by and during intervals between thunder showers. So, some sort of shelter will help us to catch fish, for it enables us to sit out the storm and take advantage of conditions which otherwise might drive us home.

But how do we take advantage? What flies are we going to use, and how? And when? Well, for a night's fishing I use five different types of lure. First is the large, slimline, silver-bodied fly I call the 'Medicine' - a long blue hackle with widgeon or brown mallard wing dressed on light, low-water salmon hooks in sizes two to six.

Next is a tiny fly, the Small Double, a drab little creature dressed on a number twelve short shank double iron. It will sometimes work wonders, either deep down or near the surface, when the sea trout refuse the Medicine or are being finicky and simply tweaking it.

Number three is the Sunk Lure - this is a tenuous creation, very slimline, but two-and-a-half to three inches in length, dressed on a tandem mount of either two short shank single hooks or two short shank doubles. It consists of two long, blue hackle feathers - one on either side - with some strands of peacock on top. Fished slowly on a sunk line it will attract sea trout of all sizes late on after midnight, when so often the fish have gone down, but it is especially good for hooking big fish. I have taken a number of sea trout of over 10 pounds on it, in addition to an occasional salmon. Indeed, this is the only lure I know that will catch salmon on pitch dark nights.

Number four is the Secret Weapon, a lure specially designed for fishing fly maggot: a number 14 or 16 treble is set half-an-inch behind a fine wire number eight single hook, which holds the maggots. There are times - particularly in low water - when the combination of fly and maggot can be very successful. The customary lure is a small, single-hook fly with two or three maggots impaled on the hook. When a sea trout takes with gusto, this arrangement is quite satisfactory since, together with the maggots, the hook is sucked inside the fish's mouth. But sea trout don't always take in such an obliging manner; some-times, usually when rain is imminent, a fish will give the maggots a tweak and let them go again, rather in the same way that a salmon will nip a prawn. All the angler feels is a series of infuriating little tugs. The Secret Weapon puts an end to this. Now, when a sea trout tweaks a maggot impaled on the main hook, it finds itself liphooked by the tiny treble lying astern.

Armed with Medicine, Small Double, Sunk Lure and Secret Weapon, we should be able to catch fish on most nights. There is, however, a notable omission from the list. This is the Surface Lure, without which no night fisherman should ever go to the river. The principle of this lure is different from that of any other type of lure; indeed, the way we fish it is the antithesis of all customary methods of fly-fishing.

When we are casting across a stream in daylight, the V-shaped wake caused by a dragging fly is something we are careful to avoid; but when fishing at night with Surface Lure, it is precisely this drag we wish to create - it can be very attractive to sea trout. Obviously, in order to produce a wake, the lure must be kept on the move. If, when being fished across a current, the line is allowed to go slack, the lure will start to drift downstream and drag will disappear. It is the wake of the lure and not the lure itself that seems to attract fish. The body of the lure, about one-and-a-half inches long, can be made either of quill plugged with cork or entirely of cork. Using doubled 24 pound nylon, a tandem mount is prepared about two-and-a-half inches long with single hook and a treble on the tail. The body of the lure is whipped to the single hook leaving the treble trailing an inch or so behind. Colour and dressing are unimportant. What the lure must do is float. A large, well-oiled, fuzzy fly such as a Loch Ordie can be effective, especially in the half-light or when there is a moon behind the clouds. Sea trout will take the surface lure at any hour of the night, but the most likely period is after midnight has struck on a warm, cloudy night without moon or stars. All holding water is worth trying so long as the surface is calm enough for the lure to leave a wake. Strangely enough, the success of this lure varies from season to season. Some years it catches me a lot of sea trout, in others very few. Even so, it is capable of attracting the biggest fish in the pool when other methods have failed.

The Surface Lure has a double function; it not only hooks fish, it indicates where the fish are lying. Many sea trout will simply splash at the lure without taking it. Knowing their position we can, if we wish, go to work on them with something else; but such tactics are seldom used until late at night. When starting to fish at dusk we choose an appropriate size of fly, say a number 4 Medicine.

Choice of fly is one thing, method of fishing it entirely another. There are two fundamentally different ways of fishing a fly: on or near the surface and close to the bottom. Both methods involve a number of variations, nevertheless they may all be placed under two headings - floating line and sunk line. The hour or so of dusk often inspires a burst of sea trout activity during which the fish tend to rise to a fly fished near the surface. This means that for part of the night at least we can fish profitably with a floating line - an altogether delightful method. Indeed, sometimes we can continue to do so with success all night. Far more often, however, we can't. On those nights when the temperature takes a dive after dark and a chill ground mist blankets the river, fish no longer show much inclination to rise; seemingly intent only on their breathing, they lie in the deeper water and remain indifferent to a fly that passes high overhead. You may wonder why they should take a fly at all late on a cold night. The answer is that, with the exception of a Surface Lure which may tempt an occasional fish to come to the top, they won't unless we fish deep and slow. On many nights therefore, in order to give ourselves the best chance of catching fish, we should be prepared to fish a fly fairly fast and close to the surface at dusk and later - when the fish have gone down - to fish it slowly, close to the bottom. This means that since both floating line and sunk line tactics are likely to be used during the same night, our minimum tackle requirements will be a suitable fly rod and two lines - floating line and sinking line. A better arrangement - to save messing about in the dark changing reels - is to use two rods, one fitted with a floater, the other with a sinker. In which case there's little point in using rods of different types. The Surface Lure will be fished on the floating line as well as the fly and only a strong rod will punch a Surface Lure out against the wind - and an equally powerful rod will be needed for fishing the big Sunk Lure on a high density line.

A reel is simply a revolving drum that can hold a fly line with as much backing as a fish is likely to take out; nevertheless, it's a very important piece of tackle, as the novice appreciates when his first big fish sets off at speed. To anyone who hasn't experienced it before, the power of a really big sea trout is astonishing, not to say alarming, and if the fish sets off down the pool there is nothing that can be done to stop it. If you try to check that first rush you will be broken - and I'm not going to qualify that statement. I've known it happen too often to too many people; which is why, if you're going to fish Sunk Lure on a high density line late at night, when you're most likely to hook a big fish, you'll need plenty of backing and a strong leader. For myself, I never fish a big Sunk Lure on a leader of under 14 or 15 pounds breaking strain. This may sound heavy for sea trout, but I have been very glad of it when a double-figure fish has taken me in a strong current on a long sunk line and gone screaming off in the darkness.

To help you land a big fish you need a big net. A small net will only land a small fish and sooner or later it will let you down. Get something simple and strong with a great big wide mouth. To help you fiddle with your tackle at night, some sort of flashlamp is essential. The best place for it when you want to use it is in your mouth; this leaves both hands free and the beam can be directed exactly where you wish. Of course, a light should never be flashed on the water you are fishing. When you want to change a fly or unravel a tangle, keep well away from the river and turn your back on it. For night fishing, in addition to the lures and tackle already mentioned, you will need some spare nylon, a priest - a bag for carrying fish - a pair of scissors and a bottle of midge repellent - and whatever else you forget, don't let it be that.

A typical fishing night may be split up into three periods: from dusk until approximately midnight, from midnight until - say - one o'clock in the morning and from then until daylight. The first period, to use a sporting metaphor, I call 'the first half', the second period 'half time' and the third period 'the second half'. There's also a brief period at daybreak that will sometimes produce a fish or two and I call that 'extra time'. It will be found that roughly 60% of the fish caught during a season's fishing will be taken in the first half, about 10% during half time and about 30% during the second half and extra time - but it's worth noting that the second half provides a bigger average size of fish. Of course, these figures must not be taken too literally; they are intended only as an indication of what to expect. On some nights, fish may be caught only during the first hour, on others not until perhaps two or three o'clock in the morning. Very occasionally, the fish may stay on the take from dusk all through the night, but such nights are rare indeed, the weather conditions being what they are in these islands. But whatever the conditions, there will be a much better chance of catching fish if we have some idea of where they're lying or likely to be lying. This comes partly from experience and partly from careful daylight reconnaissance - and I mean careful. Always creep up to the waterside, taking advantage of cover; and move slowly - few fish are easily seen. The grey shapes lying like ghosts against the shingle blend with their surroundings; to detect them takes practice, so take your time, and don't stand up. In sunshine it is the shadows of the fish you are likely to notice first. In some rivers, fish are impossible to spot, in which case you can spend some profitable minutes watching the current with its swirls and eddies and trying to pinpoint probable lies. And, at dusk in low water, keep your ears open for the sound of running fish. Early in the season, no matter how low the river, some sea trout will come splashing up as soon as darkness falls.

These astonishing night-runs of sea trout are very exciting. The fish come zipping up through the shallows then splash over the sill of the weir and glide on into the deeper water above. Although the river is far too low for salmon to run, either by day or by night, sea trout force their way up from pool to pool through stickles only a few inches deep. But the majority of the sea trout, together with the returning summer salmon, are waiting in the estuary for a rise of water. Suddenly, the tired river starts to dance and sparkle with a new flush of oxygen, and the moment is seized. When you hear the splash of sea trout running at dusk, you can look forward to some sport later that night when the fish have reached their resting pools. But except for these running fish, sea trout don't move about a lot at night. When we go down at dusk to fish over a shoal of sea trout located during the day, we may confidently expect them to be lying where we saw them and we have every chance of success. Every chance, that is, if they're not frightened.

While dusk turns to darkness, we must fish with extra care. Once it is dark sea trout may accept a faulty cast, but no disturbance of any kind will be tolerated until the shadows have lengthened considerably. When it has become difficult to see the pitch of the fly, we start by fishing a Medicine down to the head of the shoal - letting the leading fish see the fly but trying to prevent the line from passing over them. This can be done provided the position of the shoal has been lined up with some prominent feature on the opposite bank. The moment a fish is hooked, we walk him upstream so he can be played and landed well clear of the others. Fish after fish can sometimes be taken in this manner if we cast skilfully enough and move, both on the bank and in the water, as quietly as a ghost. As the night darkens we can move on down the pool and fish out the tail before the first half comes to an end. With the exception of those clear, cold evenings of swirling ground mist when the temperature drops sharply with the setting sun and we may start by fishing deep, floating line tactics are likely to be in operation during the first half.

That sea trout usually take best of all during this period, there can be no argument and there are few fishermen who will not agree that after some exciting action, lasting for anything from half an hour to, say, an hour-and-a-half, the sea trout stop taking and go down. This sudden cessation of sea trout activity is the start of what I call 'half time' and there is never any doubt when it happens. The fish themselves blow the whistle and the river seems suddenly lifeless. It is at this point that so many people lose heart. Thinking the fish are off for the night, they take their tackle apart and go home. They may be right, but on 19 evenings out of 20, they will be wrong. Without doubt the fish are down and the chances are that they will stay down, but that doesn't mean they can't be caught. Indeed, on most nights the fly fisherman has the chance of catching sea trout at any time until daybreak - and after - provided he changes his tactics in sympathy with the sea trout's change of behaviour.

As I said earlier, over a season the period after midnight will produce the bigger fish. This is because our tactics during the second half consist mainly of Sunk Lure and Surface Lure fishing, and these methods sometimes tempt a big fish that a smaller lure has failed to move. That the period we need to fish deep with a Sunk Lure should also be propitious for Surface Lure may seem contradictory, but darkness is all-important for surface fishing and on many nights early in the season, it's never really dark until after midnight. This is not to imply that all big fish are caught late at night. I mean only that you have a better chance of catching a whopper after than before midnight. You may not, of course, ever catch one at all, but if anything I say gives you the incentive to put on a sinking line and fish on into the night after other fishermen have gone home, I shall at least have helped you to take the first step towards landing one. As well as the chance of a big sea trout in the early hours, there is also the chance of a salmon. I have taken quite a few salmon with a two-and-a-half to three inch Sunk Lure in low, clear water late at night, and so have several of my friends. In all, eight different rivers have been involved. I am not referring to mid-summer twilight fishing, but really dark nights from mid-July onwards. The taking times have been between one o'clock and about three-thirty. If there was a moon, thick cloud has covered it, although one well-remembered, fourteen-pounder did take in moonlight diffused by high cirrus. Temperature seeems to have little effect. On several occasions I have caught salmon when the river was shrouded in ground mist.

Wherever I fish at night now, my approach is much the same. The repertoire of Small Double, Medicine and Surface Lure on floating line with Sunk Lure and secret Weapon on sinking line provide sport on most fishable nights of the season. Provided there are fish in the water, it is seldom that these lures are fished all night without success. And the results of success are long-lasting. Contrary to what I have been told, sea trout deep-freeze very well provided they are in top condition. At Cragg, we keep only the early season fish, straight from the sea with tide lice on them. The fish is wetted, placed in a polythene bag and taped up with its weight and date of capture written on the parcel. For me, a sea trout from the deep freeze at Christmas is something of a ritual: to admire the fish once more, to read its details on the label and look them up in my fishing diary adds another dimension to the pleasure of catching it.

Sea Trout, Darkness and the Sunk Lure
(from *The Angler's Annual* 1966)
A dark mid-August night with a heavy tumble of cloud and a hint of

rain. The little river at summer low and running crystal clear over its pale grey stones. A brown owl hooting from the wooded fellside; another from a spinney at my back. No other sound - except a whisper of wind in the leaves and a faint chuckle of water from the run-in at the head of the pool.

Two o'clock in the morning. I was alone, sitting on the bank, smoking, my rod propped up against a bush. In the fish-bag hanging from a tree branch, five sea trout; all caught between dusk and 11 p.m. Since then, nothing. Not an offer. Not even the movement of a fish.

There was an early morning chill in the air. With thoughts of hot coffee and whisky I debated whether to pack up and go home. The light from my cottage kitchen winked invitingly from the distant fell.

And then, with dramatic suddenness, a heavy splash - somewhere out in the darkness to my left, up near the head of the pool.

"Slosh," would fit it better. The sound a big fish makes when it lunges once on the surface before sinking back to its lie. The first really big fish to move that night. I could guess to a foot where it had risen: by a sunken rock under some sycamore branches on the far bank. An age-old lie for a big sea trout.

Ripples lapped the shingle at my feet, then all was quiet again. Thoughts of coffee and whisky had vanished. I took my rod and retired behind some bushes. Torch in mouth, I cut off the fly I had been using - a number three Mallard & Silver - and tied on the big Sunk Lure: a slender, tenuous thing of peacock herl and blue, three inches long.

To attack at once when a big fish moves is always a great temptation - and a great mistake. I sucked the Lure, tested the knot, then sat down and lit another cigarette.

The Lure, by the way, is called "Sunk" not because it is always fished deep down near the bottom (although it often is), but to distinguish it from the surface Lure which is made of cork and fished only on the surface, never beneath.

When the cigarette had burned down, I stubbed it out and walked softly up the shingle to the head of the pool. Well upstream, clear of

Early photographs from the 1950's. Above, HF with a salmon in Scotland and right, at Knott End with a fine sea trout taken on the spinning rod

the "Sycamore" lie, I started to fish.

Not for the big chap. Not yet. Just practice casts to make sure everything was working as it should. The fish was lying in about five feet of water. I wanted my Lure swimming horizontally a foot below the surface and moving at just the right speed and angle as it passed across his field of vision. Nothing very difficult in that. I knew the strength of current and the length of line needed to cover him.

When everything was going smoothly, I moved very quietly downstream and made the all-important cast. The line hissed in the air. The Lure went out into the bushy darkness, touched down, sank, and started to swing ...

The big fish took it at once.

A feeling of ... not surprise. I had hooked other big sea trout on the Sunk Lure in low water late at night after hearing them move, some of them in that very lie. A sense, rather, of wonderment ... once again the trick had actually worked!

Anyway, there he was. Well hooked and rushing about. No snags in that pool, so it was just a question of time. He kept on the go and did most of the work himself. In about 15 minutes he was ready to land.

I knew he was a mighty fine fish, 14 or 15lb, so I didn't take any risks. I walked him to some deep slack water, sank the big net, its handle held between my legs, and waited until I saw the faint gleam of his flank before drawing him gently in . . .

Beside the fishing shelter behind the bushes, I stretched him out on the grass and put the light on him. I nearly dropped the torch. He wasn't a sea trout at all. He was a salmon!

That happened many years ago. It was the first salmon I had ever caught with fly on a dark night. I have caught a few since then, though!

I am not going to argue the definition of a "dark" night. It was dark. But when I say "fly" you will understand what I mean. It wasn't a fly. It was the big Sunk Lure, three inches of it, that hooked the salmon. Altogether, it was a very exciting moment. Because I knew I was on to something.

Of course, I wasn't fishing for a salmon. What I thought I was fishing for was a big sea trout.

Well, dear reader, if you are one of those fishermen who believes that sea trout in a river behave like brown trout, and that their "taking" times correspond to times of actual feeding - and it is surprising how many people do - you will be wondering what I was doing fishing for sea trout in a small, low, clear river with a three inch Sunk Lure.

The answer is that to me it is the logical size of lure to use. For one thing, I don't believe that sea trout take my Lure - or anything else I tie on - because they are feeding , because I know very well that they are not. Not in my river, whatever they may do in yours. Nor in any other sea trout river I have ever fished. Although, of course, I haven't fished every sea trout river; and there may be rivers where the sea trout feed like mad. But I haven't come across them.

It is very possible that one of my more naive readers, who firmly believes that sea trout feed and I am insane, may fish on a river where there is a considerable hatch of fly and the sea trout do indulge in occasional orgies. If so, he will, I assume, offer the fish an imitation of whatever they are taking. Probably a sedge , or something of that sort. But the question I should like to pose is this: What is his philosophy when there is no hatch of fly; when the night turns cold and the river seems empty, and the ground mist swirls round his legs like smoke? What will he do then? Take his rod to pieces and go home?

You think this is a *reductio ad absurdum*?

Listen. In an article not long ago, some fellow traveller stated categorically: " The only time worth fishing for sea trout is when the fish are on the feed. Otherwise," as he put it, "you might as well pack up." Well - anyone who will believe that will believe anything.

I can assure any other fisherman not already aware of it that the total absence of a hatch of fly, or any sign of feeding fish, will have little effect on his fishing chances. Indeed, if his approach to sea trout fishing and the flies he uses are based on the idea of a feeding fish, he is denying himself all but a fractional chance of success - especially with big fish.

Most of the sea trout I have ever fished for did not take food - which is quite a lot of fish, because I have been after them for nearly 40 years. Nevertheless, I do not suggest that no sea trout ever takes food. No, no. But there is a very important distinction between "taking food" and "feeding". And pray do not immediately condemn this statement as mere casuistry, dear reader, because it isn't - as we shall see.

After their pelagic tour, most sea trout return to the rivers in which they were born. Not all of them; most of them. And since the habits of various colonies of the pure species of fish often differ according to their environment, one would expect sea trout (and salmon), after generations of breeding in rivers of different character, to display different characteristics; and frequently they do.

In some rivers sea trout will take a certain amount of food, if it is available. In others, nothing at all. But sea trout have no need of food. Like salmon, they are equipped by nature to withstand a prolonged fast while in fresh water; and although their behaviour may vary according to their environment, and although, in consequence, some may avail themselves of occasional snacks, very few, if any, sea trout can reasonably be termed feeding fish.

Several hundreds of adult sea trout (I am not referring anywhere in this article to herling or immature sea trout) come into my cottage every summer, some fresh from sea, some after varying periods of river life. We examine the stomach contents of a great many of these fish. And what do we find? Nothing.

Well - that statement is not quite in accordance with the facts. In the 350-odd adult sea trout examined last year, five items of food were found: three fly larvae, one caterpillar, and the remains of one unidentifiable creepy-crawly. No fish contained more than one item. So that out of 350 fish, only five had anything at all inside them. And as that can be taken as being representative of food I have found in sea trout over the years, you will understand why I base my fishing philosophy on the idea of "habit"!

I concede that each of those five had enjoyed a tiny meal. But I feel it is going a little too far to claim that because they had swallowed one little creature apiece, they were feeding ! So far as the others are concerned, the argument doesn't arise. They didn't have anything in them at all.

Briefly, the brown trout takes food in order to live. Without that food the fish would die. Therefore, it feeds. But the sea trout when it is in the river, has no such need of sustenance; and although some may rise to nymph, or to a hatch of fly, they are not feeding in the same sense of the word. And indeed, the loss of condition factor of those that do take food remains unaffected.

That is the fundamental difference between sea trout and brown trout physiology, and it demands from the sea trout fisherman a fundamental difference of approach.

In my experience, the concept of a non-feeding fish which takes because of habit, and not because of hunger and necessity, is a very sound basis from which to start thinking about how to catch sea trout. Empirically, it leads to something like the Sunk Lure.

For all I know, the country may be seething with sea trout fishermen who have been fishing at night all their lives with great big flies like the Sunk Lure. If so, I ask their indulgence. It is just that we have never met. So far as I am concerned, I thought the thing out for myself - and when I started to fish it, even my friends laughed. They laugh no longer.

The reasons why I thought this type of lure would be so successful demand considerably more space than this article can afford; anyone who is interested can find something about them in my book: *Sea Trout Fishing*. I should say at once that some of them are rather shaky. Nevertheless, however wonky my theories may have been, they led to three very successful results: one of which was the Sunk Lure.

Mind you, when that book was written I didn't know as much about the Sunk Lure as I do now. I had discovered it was good at night, especially for big fish, when the river was up a bit and conditions generally were difficult. But I now know that it is very good for all sizes of fish; not only when the river is up a bit, but sometimes when it is dead low as well. On many occasions it has had great success on nights when few other fish have been caught. In addition, of course, to hooking salmon!

So, although I can imagine that its efficacy may well vary from river to river, it is a lure which most night fly-fishermen might find it worth their while to try. And I pass the idea on to you with my compliments.

After all, I am sure it has already crossed your minds that if the Sunk Lure will catch double-figure sea trout in the river I fish, there is at least a fleeting chance it might do so in yours, too. Besides, there is this interesting business of the salmon.

Why aren't more salmon caught late on dark nights? Is it because so few people fish for them? I have an idea that, except at dusk and dawn, the orthodox sea trout fisherman fails to catch them because his flies are too small. They are often too small to catch the very big sea trout, too!

Perhaps I am wrong. There may be numerous instances of salmon taking a small fly on a pitch-dark night. But it hasn't happened within my experience. I am not, of course, referring to mid-summer twilight fishing in low water on Scottish salmon rivers; but dark nights from mid-July onwards, when on occasion there has also been a thick blanket of ground mist.

The river I fish mostly nowadays is a small sea trout beck. It holds salmon; but they are few and far between. I sometimes wonder what might be done at night with Sunk Lure on a major salmon river. And any reader who wishes to experiment might be interested to know the conditions which have so far attended every instance of my catching salmon at night.

The taking time has been after midnight, between approximately 1.30 and 3.30 p.m.

The night has been dark. If a moon, then thick cloud has covered it - although one salmon took in diffused light from high cirrus.

On several occasions there has been thick ground mist, with accompanying drop in temperature. The river has been low and clear.

The fish has been lying in from six feet of water, usually near the head of a pool. The Lure has been moving fairly quickly, a foot to 18 inches below the surface: a Sunk Lure, two-and-a-half to three inches.

In every case, the fish has moved shortly before it took.

That this taking fish was the fish that moved is, of course, only an assumption. But although there is no absolute proof, I am certain in my own mind they were one and the same. Nevertheless, perhaps it would be more accurate to say: On no occasion have I caught a salmon in these circumstances when a fish had not moved shortly beforehand, in the same position as, or very close to, the fish that took.

CHAPTER 15

TOM RAWLING ON THE FALKUS METHOD

Corner pool

Fish all Night for the Big Fish

The hook came out in the net, but the sea trout was safely mine. Back from the river, in the light of my torch, I found where the hook had been. A little red nick in the very front of the lower jaw: a hold typical of the early-season fish. Just one more jump and perhaps he would have been off. But a fisherman needs his luck: my fish hadn't made a final flurry and I was proud to have caught him. The first fish of the season, on this the earliest of beats.

Nobody else had even wetted a line. The river was dead low. This was the one pool known to be holding sea trout, and only four fish had been seen in it!

Just a few minutes earlier, I had been sheltering in the broom bushes beside the pool, when a fish 'moved' - over by the rocks, I thought. I finished my cigarette, giving him time to settle back in his lie. Then, I put a big lure across him. He took it, first cast. And now, here he was, shimmering in the spotlight of my torch. It was a great moment.

A silver lining to my own dark cloud, for a family bereavement had brought me North. Tired and tense, I could not sleep in the empty house, and I had come to Cragg Cottage for companionship with no thoughts of fishing. Warm by the crackling log-fire, we talked on into the night while outside a cold wind rattled the back kitchen door. Then Kathleen went to bed and Hugh got out his typewriter - he had a deadline and was going to work all night. He refilled my glass: I was at ease. And then, I found myself thinking idly of those four sea trout that Hugh had mentioned during supper. The first fish of a new season... silvery-fresh from the sea... beautiful...desirable. They tempted me.

I remembered that my box of lures was in the car. I thought about the lures and those four sea trout...Why not? And so, at length, although it was long after midnight, out I went with a borrowed rod. A keen blustery wind was ruffling the pool. There was so little current that I had to draw line by hand to make the line work. Only four fish in the beat, and it was already morning. By all the books on sea trout fishing, I was crazy!

By all the books save one.

That book is *Sea Trout Fishing* - A Guide To Success by Hugh Falkus (Witherby 1962). Without knowledge of the concept of night fly fishing for sea trout advanced by Falkus and several seasons of trying to put it into practice, I should never have dreamed of going down to the river to catch a trout at half-past one in the morning, let alone in such adverse conditions. Of all the writers on sea trout fishing, only Falkus gives more than a glance at the possibility of such an unorthodox outing being successful. For him, it is an integral part of his entirely new concept of sea trout fishing.

New indeed; startlingly so. For the first time in angling literature, sea trout fishing is conceived as being neither a branch of brown trout nor of salmon fishing, but as a sport entirely of its own, with its own strategy, tactics and techniques based on a new understanding of sea trout behaviour.

The concept may be summarised as follows:-

1. Sea trout in rivers do not 'feed' in the accepted sense of the word. The approach to sea trout fishing therefore is not founded, as hitherto, on the idea of a fish that 'takes' because it is hungry and in search of food.

2. Sea trout in the river exhibit a strange but distinct pattern of behaviour. From dusk to midnight or thereabouts, they are often willing to 'take' near the surface. After this, the fish go 'down' and the river seems lifeless. Nevertheless, there are chances right through until dawn, even in very poor conditions (eg ground-mist, low temperature, full moon etc), when sea trout can be 'induced' to take by techniques completely different from those used hitherto.

3. In the main, success late at night demands a variety of sunk line methods - to which, the Surface or Wake Lure is an important exception. Late night fishing not only offers excellent chances of catching sea trout, but provides many of the biggest fish. Hence, Falkus advises all who want to catch big sea trout to fish all night, irrespective of weather conditions, except when the river is in spate and the water is coloured. This is what he says:

'Fish all night, if free to do so. Don't give up because the sea trout have gone down or your bag is still empty at one o'clock in the morning. Poor conditions can be defeated if their reactions on the fish are studied and understood. You will get an "offer" at some time during the night. Perhaps only the one, and you may have to fish hard to get it, but that one may be from the best fish of the season.

Boldly he states his conclusion:

'There are few fishing nights during a season when sea trout cannot be caught.'

This is an astonishing statement: the touchstone of his whole concept. Nothing remotely like it has been said before. If it really works, his approach to sea trout night fly fishing represents the most remarkable angling discovery for many decades, comparable only with Wood's discovery of greased line fishing for salmon.

In my experience it does work. And in consequence, my pleasure and interest in sea trout fishing have been immeasurably increased.

But if one may judge from the angling press, Falkus's discoveries have not yet been understood, let alone put into practice, except by a few fishermen lucky enough to fish the Cumberland Esk with him, on his own water at Cragg Cottage. These fishermen - and I am one of them - have tested and proved the Falkus approach. My reason for writing this article is to encourage other sea trout fishermen to do the same on their waters. But first, I suggest, they should understand and appreciate the originality of what Falkus has written, and be prepared to question conventional methods.

Falkus has said it all with great clarity in his book. Very few fishermen make any entirely new discovery, and still fewer successfully communicate it. Falkus has done both. Anyone who doubts his originality can soon check with the generally accepted authorities. It will not take long: there are few books that deal at length with fly fishing at night for sea trout in rivers. None of them is truly relevant to the Falkus thesis, since the authors rarely, if ever, seem to have fished all through the night. For example, R.C. Bridgett in *Sea-trout Fishing* says: 'My experience of night-fishing cannot be claimed as extensive'; Jeffrey Bluett in *Sea trout and Occasional Salmon* states: 'I have not fished all through the night a great number of times'; and F.W. Holiday in *River-Fishing for Sea Trout*, published as recently as 1960, declares: 'Night-fishing, generally speaking, is between the hours of sunset and midnight. Very occasionally you may fish hopefully all night ... you may be lucky enough to hit on two or three such nights in a whole summer.'

Nowhere have I been able to find anything like the Falkus concept - not even in Dame Juliana Berners! Yet the reviewers of Falkus's book were, at the best, lukewarm in praise. Perhaps the outspoken challenge to traditional dogma was so revolutionary that it was bound to produce a response of incredulity.

I confess that when I first read the pre-publication extracts from Falkus's book in *The Fishing Gazette*, I had doubts.But there was a power and a certainty in the book as a whole that urged me to write to the author. Soon I was invited to fish with him, and at once discovered what a magnificent fisherman he is. So outstanding in concentration, perception, and technique, that as I struggled to understand and learn a new way of fishing, I often wondered if his methods were transferable to others of only average ability.

Slowly I learned the techniques, and the water; gradually I began to understand what he was talking about. It was hard work, both mentally and physically, but competence and confidence grew and fed on each other, until in my third summer holiday at Cragg Cottage the fish began to respond to the sunk line technique in the small hours. Nowadays, whenever I can, whatever the conditions, I fish all through the night, for I have found that my own catches follow the Falkus pattern.

This is the pattern, as he describes it:

'A fishing night may be split up into three periods; from dusk until approximately midnight: from midnight until, say, one o'clock in the morning; and from then until daylight. The first period we will call - to use a sporting metaphor - the "first-half"; the second period, "half-time"; and the third period, the "second-half."

It will be found that roughly 60 percent of the fish caught during a season's night fishing will be taken in the 'first-half'; about 10 per cent during "half-time"; and about 30 percent during the "second-half". But it is worth noting that the second-half will provide many of the big fish that are caught.'

And I have found this to be so. My own records of adult sea trout caught, show a similar pattern: 54 percent in the "first-half"; 12 per cent during half-time; and after that, in the second-half, 34 per cent. Almost as many fish after midnight as before. And, in addition, the average weight is heavier after than before midnight, by a full pound, for the second-half has brought me most of my biggest fish.

Of course my numbers of fish are relatively small - I think I've done well if I have 30 to 40 fish in my holiday fortnight - but the pattern is unmistakably the same as that described by Falkus. There are few nights when I haven't caught fish. Also, the other guests at Cragg Cottage can produce similar confirmation. Each night's fishing is always fully discussed and recorded. Once a guest becomes competent in understanding and technique, his catches begin to conform to the Falkus pattern, with the biggest fish usually caught long after midnight.

Techniques to induce big fish to take
The reader may object that my experience is mainly on one river and that the behaviour of sea trout in other rivers is quite different. But such first-class fishermen as Brigadier G.H.N. Wilson, Dr Jimmy Skene, Mr Michael Marshall, and others, have told me of their success with Falkus methods on other rivers - Border Esk, Cumberland Derwent, Irt, Lancashire Leven, Lune, Crake, Cothi, Towy and Torridge.

It may be claimed that Falkus methods do not work on all rivers; but they certainly work on all rivers where Falkus and his friends have had the chance to use them. And by 'work', I mean not only catch fish, but succeed when traditional methods have failed!

When considering these apparent differences in sea trout behaviour in various rivers, it is important to remember that the behaviour I am discussing is elicited in response to certain types of lures presented in certain ways. The type of stimulus, the method of fishing, is of crucial importance.

I would suggest that the fisherman for whom Falkus's methods do not work has probably applied them without conviction. He has failed to understand, or has not accepted the whole approach from which the methods spring.

A fisherman's approach to sea trout fishing is determined by his conception of sea trout behaviour; in particular, by his acceptance or rejection of the hypothesis that sea trout feed in freshwater.

As a consequence of their belief in fresh water feeding, most anglers fish for sea trout as if they were brown trout, with flies that are considered to be representations of insects found in that particular river. Many of the 'flies' are clearly small-fish imitations, though this is not always admitted.

Both these types of 'flies' are usually fished on a 'floating' line just under the surface, as in traditional wet-fly fishing, with success from dusk until midnight, or so. When the fish go 'down,' the conventional explanation is given - significantly, in brown trout terms. The 'rise' is over, the fish are 'off,' and the fisherman might as well go home to bed. It may be that some thoughtful anglers have realised that nymphs and small fish are not always found just under the surface, and that sea trout might be 'feeding' deep, but F.W. Holiday roundly declares: 'Almost all fly-fishing for sea trout is now (1960) done with a greased or floating line and this is the only method which will be discussed.'

Only Bluett, of the recognised sea trout authors I have read, discusses sunk-line fishing, although he does it with purist reluctance. My reading of his book leads me to think that though he was a good fisherman and an alert observer, he was blinkered by his belief that sea trout, when in rivers, behave exactly like brown trout.

So, to put it very briefly, the upshot of the belief in 'feeding in freshwater' is that fisherman give up at midnight, or before when they consider sea trout have stopped feeding.

Now to Falkus, who affirms that sea trout in freshwater do not feed in the accepted sense of the word, ie because they are hungry and search for food. He has unrivalled opportunities to observe sea trout (and salmon) every day they are in the river. He is a highly-skilled observer, with an international reputation for the television films he has made in the field of bird, animal, and fish behaviour. Writing in *Angler's Annual* 1966 he states his case, with characteristic force and lucidity. I quote a key passage:

'I do not suggest that no sea trout ever takes food. No, no. But there is a very important distinction between 'taking food' and 'feeding'. '

'In some rivers sea trout will take a certain amount of food, if it is available. In others, nothing at all. But sea trout have no need of food.

Like salmon they are equipped by nature to withstand a prolonged fast while in fresh water; and although their behaviour may vary according to their environment, and although, in consequence, some may avail themselves of occasional snacks, very few, if any, sea trout can reasonably be termed feeding fish.'

So much for Falkus. Now for my own experience. Every day of my holiday, I make a 'recce' of the river. Except during a spate, the water is crystal clear, the grey-green shingle bottom is lined with sized ranks of sea trout (and here and there a salmon - you can see the concave tail fin in this transparent water). It is wonderfully exciting and instructive to peer through the alders at this great flotilla. Some fish bear scars and can be recognised as individuals - almost old friends at the end of a fortnight! Occasionally, a fish will flash its side or move a few yards, but soon it glides back onto station.

Insects on the water are almost entirely ignored. So, too, are experimental offerings of worms and maggots. Occasionally, if the watcher persists, a salmon or sea trout can be tempted to intercept one of these many offerings - as it can an artificial lure. But such fish are rare exceptions. How different from the hungry parr and brown trout, snapping at all that comes their way. They are feeding. But the sea trout and salmon lie motionless, save for a lazy fanning of the tail.

The sea trout are not feeding, yet they take a lure. Sometimes, especially when the 'offers' are very tentative, I have wondered if the fish were merely investigating this strange object moving across their field of vision. Be that as it may, however, Falkus suggests that although it declines in strength as time passes, the habit of sea-feeding persists in freshwater. Hence, sea trout can be stimulated to take a lure that gives the impression of a creature on which they have recently fed in the sea - usually an imitation of a fish. And so, for most of his fishing he uses lures, and these vary in length from between 1¼ and 3¼ inches.

In the early part of the night, he fishes these lures near the surface (common ground here, at least about depth), but after midnight when the fish go 'down' (and even before, on the nights when the fish are never 'up'), Falkus does not allow himself to be persuaded that the sea trout are not 'feeding,' and that, therefore, he might just as well stop trying to catch them. On the contrary, he continues to fish. And with mainly sunk-line techniques he is not only able to induce sea trout to take, but frequently to catch the biggest fish of the night. I have seen him do it, many times.

Few nights when you can't tempt the sea trout
Method, theory, and fish behaviour - put them in any order you like - all react with and influence each other in a complex way, far more subtle than I have been able to show. Theory does not come whole out of anyone's head; we are all heirs to tradition and to other men's knowledge; no one starts from 'square one'. Discovery comes when the fisherman finds that accepted theory is inconsistent with his own observations; when, out of his own experience and thought he creates a new hypothesis; and devises practical fishing experiments to put it to the test.

Results of these experiments, including negative results, amend the theory and suggest further experiments; and so ad infinitum. This is the empirical method of science. It comprises accurate observation and skilful experimentation, and the intuitive flash that lights up a new experimental path to original theory. From our many discussions, I know that Hugh Falkus claims an intuitive understanding of fish behaviour. But it is intuition based on painstaking observation.

He is still experimenting, for there is much more yet to be discovered. Why for example, does the Surface or Wake Lure do best in the darkest hours, at a time when the fish are 'down'? Is the wide variety of sea trout response to this floating lure a pointer to what goes on also, deep down, in sunk-line fishing?

I have enjoyed my part in the later Cragg Cottage experiments; each season a new problem. For instance, in 1968 an almost unprecedented Lake District drought shrank the river until it was two inches below the bottom of the gauge. The sea trout were cooped up in deep, sluggish pools - very difficult fishing indeed. And yet we were successful with the big Sunk Lure, a well-tried killer in high clear water

Daytime reconnaissance, Hazel Dub.

following a spate. Of course it had to be fished in a different way, discovered by experiment. One happy night, the experiment brought me a bonny six-pounder, hours after midnight, in dead low water.

And always, at the end of a night's fishing, it has been good to 'unwind' in the snug cottage kitchen with mugs of tea and whisky; and to talk over that night's sea trout problems, while through the open doorway we have watched the swiftly changing morning sky catch fire over Scafell Pike.

As Falkus is the first to agree, the pattern of sea trout behaviour is undoubtedly more intricate than the broad division - 'first-half', 'second-half' - that he describes. To increase our understanding, we must extend and deepen our observations and experiments. The Falkus theory gives full scope to experimentation with all sizes of lures, on both floating and sunk lines, all through the night. On the other hand, it seems that most anglers who have accepted sea trout as 'feeding' fish, are inhibited by their belief from trying out a full range of methods. They restrict themselves to small flies and lures on floating lines, and abandon the game at half-time.

I suggest that many of the reported differences in sea trout behaviour in various rivers, are largely a reflection of the behaviour of fishermen who regard sea trout as being indistinguishable from brown trout. Perhaps these fishermen have good day-time fishing and have neither time nor energy to spend on all-night fishing.

Again, on some rivers the salmon is accorded such superiority (often expressed in £'s), that a sea trout taking a lure is cursed as an interfering nuisance; and any man who proposed an all-night expedition for sea trout would be regarded as a potential poacher.

Volumes have been written on salmon fishing and brown trout fishing, but the specialist literature on sea trout fishing is small. This is a measure of how little serious attention has been given to sea trout fishing as a sport in its own right.

If fishermen tackled their sport empirically, I believe they would discover a greater uniformity in the behaviour of sea trout in different rivers than has yet been established. I would be surprised if those who made the effort to understand and apply Falkus's methods did not find the fish conforming to his pattern of behaviour on whatever river they were fishing. And, in consequence, they would suffer fewer blank nights.

The statement by Falkus that 'there are few fishing nights during a season when sea trout cannot be caught' is the boldest challenge of all; the nub of his book. It is important that it should be properly understood. It assumes the reader's competence as a practical night fisherman, and the use of a full range of methods.

The statement does not mean that there will be no nights when the fishing bag is empty, although, for himself on his own water, that has been the case whenever I have fished with him. He is not denying that on some nights sea trout are difficult to catch - indeed, extremely difficult. But he does mean that there are few nights when sea trout cannot be tempted to respond; to make an 'offer'. And if a fish 'offers', even in the most tentative way, then it is catchable, although the fisherman may have to work hard in varying the stimulus before he induces a more positive response.

Since I became competent in approach and methods, under Falkus's influence, I have had few nights without a measure of success. I would have had many more blank nights if I had allowed poor conditions to persuade me that an empty bag was inevitable. And, once I had experienced the thrill of catching a big sea trout late at night after hours of effort, I knew that it was possible to do it again, and not only possible, but desirable.

Success is sweetest when the odds are against you. This is what the sport of angling is all about. As Falkus says: 'the measure of a fisherman's skill, the true meaning of success, is not the number of fish he catches when sea trout are coming eagerly to the fly, but what he can achieve on the numerous occasions when they are not.'

I agree, of course, that fishing on all through the night, mainly with a sunk line, is a matter of individual taste; and of motivation. It depends on how much you want to catch sea trout. I always want to, even if I think there are only four fish in the pool! I know, now, that

233

there is always a chance of catching one.

Let Falkus sum up: 'Some writers are of the opinion that night fishing is a chancy sport, worthwhile only in certain favourable conditions, rarely profitable after midnight, and that many blank nights may be expected. Such an opinion is not formed without reason. But it results, I venture to suggest, from a fishing technique and approach which is not so comprehensive as it might be. It is because for years I have seen so many fishermen fail - simply through missing opportunities of whose existence they seemed unaware - that this book is being written.'

He is right. Both from my own experience and from that of other fishermen, I can confirm that, although they are 'down', sea trout can be 'induced' to 'take' all through the night; indeed, it is in the small hours that many of the biggest fish are caught.

Falkus has shown that the opportunities are there. Any angler who wishes to, can take them.

1970

Sea Trout by the Book

I longed to start fishing, but although the sun had already dipped behind the Lakeland fells, I stayed hidden in the broom bushes. It was too early yet. I had a breathing space; time to enjoy the afterglow that etched the ridge against the western sky in front of me; time to listen to the music of the beck and tune in to my surroundings, and to sea trout.

It was mid June, almost the shortest night of the year. The river was low and, as my Polaroids had shown that afternoon, the main pools were holding very few fish. But in a bush-lined run just below the ford, through a gap in the alders I had glimpsed three or four square tails, tucked in by the bank where fast shallow water widened and deepened into a bay a few yards long.

Lying prone, I had watched with great desire those pearl grey tails lazily fanning the clear water to send sunlight ripples over the stony bottom. Slowly, stealthily, I edged away - one frightened flick of the tails and they would vanish behind the roots of that young sycamore undercut by spates. No fly could tempt them there.

It was a fascinating challenge for my first night of the season. To cover those fish correctly in that swift current, my fly - teal-and-blue Medicine No 4 low water hook - must sink at once and then swing across them a few inches under the surface. On a floating line it would merely skate over the lie. But a high-density line should do the trick. All this I had decided during my reconnaissance, when I had studied the lie and picked a landing place for the fish I planned to catch. That upstream eddy would be deep enough to sink my net, and there was a gap in the overhanging branches where I would be able to raise my rod - just by that patch of shingle. I had memorised it all. Distances seem so different in the dark.

Now I was by the shingle, with my tackle ready. I believed that I could hook one of those fish, but I knew the night's fishing would be short. The sky was clear: in an hour or so the moon would be rising behind me - (the worst possible situation for a night fly-fisherman). My hope lay in the bushes and trees that guarded the run. They posed a desperate threat to any careless back-cast; but they would give me cover and throw dark shadows across the water.

Brambles scraped my thorn-proof coat as I stepped down to the shingle. In the gathering dusk I could just make out the sycamore marking the bay where the sea trout were lying. It was little more than an hour to moonrise, but I forced myself to wait a few more minutes. until the distant bank dissolved into darkness.

I started to wade quietly downstream, working line out into the throat of the run. Then, with a gap behind me, I deliberately cast almost square, lengthening line a foot at a time, until I heard my lure patter on a leafy twig. It came free at a twitch. So, I had a length of the line that just spanned the river, and I could confidently search the darkest shadows. I would need several arm's length more when I began to cast at an angle downstream, but I had a basis for trial - and error, perhaps? But the risk of overcasting had to be taken. My lure must land within a foot or so of the opposite bank.

I stripped in the line, letting the coils fall, and checked lure and leader by touch. Everything has to be perfect when the first casts are made over a sea trout lie at dusk. That enchanted hour as twilight thickens into darkness is often the most productive, and tonight the short spell before moonrise would give me the best - probably my only - chance to hook a fish. Any error could ruin that opportunity.

It was time to start in earnest. With the same length of line out, I shuffled further downstream, taking care not to splash in the shallow water (so much easier to wade quietly in deep water). Here at my back I had an unbroken rank of high bushes; I concentrated hard on every detail of my steeple cast, talking myself through it:

'Cock your right wrist forward on the rod handle. Dip the rod-tip to the water. Start to draw line smoothly with your left hand to full arm's length - and lift. Reach for the sky. Right wrist solid, arm straight. Stop at the vertical, right wrist solid all the time. Pause. Drive forward and down, arm straight. Aim your thumb at a point just above the lie - and let the line in your left hand shoot away.'

The cast felt good - a clean cast, a straight line, kissing the stream. Again, a longer line, moving a pace downriver as the fly landed - a trick to slow the lure as it swings. I took another yard from the reel and cast once more. The fly ought to be fishing the lie by now.

But no offer.

Not far enough across? I pulled more off the reel and cast again. There was a slow draw on the line, split-second thoughts as I raised the rod-point: 'Damn! I've overcast! That sycamore!' Then, suddenly, the rod bent and throbbed with a plunging fish.

His downstream rush ripped yards off the reel, well past the backing splice, before I heard a loud splash. I reeled in, slowly, hoping he was on, but fearing the worst, then felt him again. With rod outstretched square across the river, I backed upstream, inviting him to follow. I used no direct pressure, only the belly of the line. He came willingly enough, stemming the current, using up his strength. He was just where I wanted him, clear of far-side snags, and of the dangerous shallows at my feet.

When he'd passed me, I recovered line and bent the rod. He ran again, but not far this time. He was tiring. The next walk brought him to the eddy, where he wallowed and showed his gleaming flank. I sank my big net deep; glanced up to check the clear space overhead; then raised my arm to slide him to the net. A quick lift and he was kicking in the meshes.

Back in the broom behind the shingle, torch in mouth, I admired my prize; a magnificent early season sea trout, upwards of 3lb, still carrying sea lice. My fly had fallen from its hold, as often happens with soft-mouthed fish fresh from the sea. Any slackening of the line as I'd played him and he'd have got away!

I checked my fly and leader, waiting a while to rest the run, smoking a cigarette, rationalising my addiction as a way of measuring five minutes.

But no longer than that! Already the glow of a rising moon was spreading across the sky. I should have to be quick if I wanted to hook another fish.

I stubbed out my cigarette and waded into the shadows still cast by the broom and alders.

As the moon rose in a cloudless sky above Raven Crag, and the river ran silver, I relaxed on the bank. With that spotlight behind me I could no longer hide from wary sea trout. The all-too-short June night's sport was spent. The magic hour had passed. Indeed, what magic! From the grass at my feet, two fish flashed in the splendour of the moon.

But as I savoured my success, I found myself remembering the time when fish like these would have defeated me; when I didn't even appreciate the problems, let alone know how to solve them - those frustrating fishless nights before I had read Hugh Falkus's *Sea Trout Fishing*: the book that changed my whole approach.

The way I'd caught my brace from the run - my 'recce' and my wait for darkness - the strategy and tactics - my concentration, stealth and confidence - all the details of technique (I could list more than 20

237

items) - everything I did, was straight from the book that, back in 1962, convinced and captivated me and brought about my friendship with the author, too. He gave his book the sub-title: A Guide to Success, and that is exactly what I have found it to be, many many times.

Some people may consider two three-pounders nothing much to shout about. I agree, if conditions are favourable and your water is full of fish. But in the exacting conditions I've just described, that brace of early sea trout covered in sea lice matched up to the true yardstick of success. I know that Hugh Falkus would have been satisfied to do as well. We've fished together many nights, in fair weather and foul. Some nights brought an easy harvest. Far more were challenging. Success was sweeter then, with every fish a hard-won triumph.

However difficult the conditions were, with the sole exception of coloured water, I have never known Hugh to fail on any night. I remember him telling me once: 'Catching sea trout is like a conjuring trick - relatively simple once you know how the trick is done.' (He might have added that there's more than one trick, and that you have to know where and when to try them!) I know the trick now, though sometimes I foozle it - a careless cast perhaps. But on that June night, in the heavily-bushed run where the only practical cast was the steeple, I'd got it absolutely right. Just like the photographs in Hugh's book.

At this point, well-read anglers may protest that there are no illustrations of the steeple cast in their copies of *Sea Trout Fishing*. Quite right, there aren't. Not in the first edition, nor in its reprint. But they are in the second edition, which I have had the good fortune to read in manuscript and which is now with the printers.

But a 24 frame high-speed sequence of the steeple cast isn't the only new thing about the second edition. There is a wealth of new material. Most notable, I think, are the new chapters on stillwater and saltwater fishing. The latter includes a fascinating account of how, as a young man, Falkus made a sea-pool, out on the open shore far from a river mouth by clearing away a quarter of an acre of sea-weed and constructing 'lies' with boulders. It took him days of hard labour - but what results!

He holds to his original tenets, but has enlarged them and widened his scope to cover all the methods he has used, by day or night, throughout the British Isles. Lures, tackle and techniques are described in great detail and illustrated with more than 100 photographs and drawings, all dove-tailed into the text.

Readers of *Trout and Salmon* were largely responsible for getting his new work written. In 1970 the magazine published an article of mine on the Falkus concept of sea trout fishing. The enthusiastic flood of letters that reached Hugh persuaded him to write a second edition. (Antony Witherby, his publisher, had wanted it for years).

Publication of the second edition will demonstrate, beyond doubt, that Hugh Falkus is a great original sea trout fisherman; and will bring the recognition denied him by most reviewers of the first edition - they failed to understand his revolutionary concept, mistaking it for mere iconoclasm. But the only valid judges are anglers who have tried Falkus' methods for themselves. Many of them have written to Hugh to tell him of their success. He takes great satisfaction from their letters, for in the first edition he gave his reason for writing, thus: 'It is because for years I have seen so many fishermen fail - simply through missing opportunities of whose existence they seemed unaware - that this book is being written.'

A simple aim it seems. But consider these words of Schopenhauer: 'The man of talent is like the marksman who hits a mark the others cannot hit; the man of genius is like the marksman who hits a mark they cannot even see,'

Exactly so, Hugh Falkus has seen new marks and shown the rest of us how to hit home. Moreover, he writes with such lucidity, zest, and rare charm, that he has created not just the definitive book on sea trout fishing, but a classic of angling literature.

1975